HEALTH CARE without CORRUPTION

An Innovative, Nonprofit Solution

By

Behzad Mohit M.D.

Published in the United States by Buckeye Press.

Printed in the United States of America.

Library of Congress Catalog-in-Publication Data
Mohit, Behzad, 1933 -
Health care without corruption: an innovative, nonprofit solution / Behzad Mohit. — 1st ed.

Includes bibliographical references.
ISBN 978-0-9895297-1-6

First Edition

To the memory of my mother, Sedi Shahroodi,

who showed me the way to love and serve people.

Acknowledgements

I AM INDEBTED TO THE ABLE AND EXTENSIVE RESEARCH OF Sangeet Duchane and Evan Winchester. My sincere thanks are also due to Mr. Winchester and Trevor Cohen for their careful editorial work. The encouragement and feedback of Dr. Lawrence Litman, Farhad Mohit, Linda Vela, and Maryam and Juliet Mohit has also been essential to the completion of this book.

Contents

A Personal Introduction

WRITING THIS BOOK HAS BEEN A LONG PROCESS, ONE THAT began decades before any of the words you are about to read were put to the page.

My mother's devotion to raising orphans off the streets inspired me to become a physician. I was intent to make her proud by helping people through medical research and treatment. However, after 50 years, I came to realize that all those late nights spent in laboratories, emergency rooms, and free clinics were perhaps only a few drops of clear water in the muddy river of our increasingly corrupt health care system. What was I to do when all I could hear was the deafeningly silent sound of passivity?

So over the last five years, in the autumn of my life, I dedicated myself to researching the systematic problems that plague our health care delivery system. After many sleepless nights, I have arisen with new energy and optimism. The book you are about to read is a shrill siren of hope. It will awaken you to the profound problems facing life's most important necessity: health care.

Fortunately, it is not too late. With knowledge and courage, we can place health back into the service of humanity. Read this book carefully for yourself, your family, and your country, and take action. Together we can put an end to the travesty of profitable illness. It is my sincere hope that as informed citizens, we will rise above greed and claim our right to health, as indispensable to "life, liberty, and the pursuit of happiness.

THE PROBLEM

How Profit can Make us Sick

Modern medicine is a negation of health. It isn't organized to serve human health, but only itself, as an institution. It makes more people sick than it heals.

– Ivan Illich, *Medical Nemesis*.[1]

A MIDDLE-AGED WOMAN WITH A WART THE SIZE OF A PEA on her middle finger walked into my dermatology office. I asked her if the growth had been treated before. "Yes, doctor," she said, "I have been going to Dr. X for eight months. Every two weeks, he freezes it and shaves it off. But the wart is still here." Over nearly a year, her insurance had spent $1,200 on the repeated treatments. In a matter of minutes, I froze the wart to its core with liquid nitrogen and in two weeks it was completely gone, at a cost of $75. The woman's insurance company had paid 16 times what the procedure should have cost. Her doctor's practice was so busy he could only accept new patients after a three month waiting period. Ironically, many patients saw the doctor's long waitlist as a sign of his expertise and clamored for his "special treatment."

K.A., a 52-year-old businessman and a good friend of mine went to see his doctor for a routine medical check-up. He was somewhat overweight and his doctor decided that he needed an angiogram to test the blood vessels in his heart. After the examination, my friend called me from the hospital. The doctors had found that his main coronary artery—the blood vessel feeding his heart—was more than 50 percent narrower than normal. They strongly recommended open heart surgery. I advised him to get a second opinion to confirm that this extensive surgery was indeed necessary. He accepted my professional advice.

The next day, K.A.'s wife called to say that her husband had just undergone successful open heart surgery. I went to visit him and indeed he seemed fine. I asked him why the rush, what happened to his promise to get a second opinion? He explained that four doctors and a nurse had surrounded him all at once and warned that if he left the hospital, it would be at his own peril.

"I got scared and did it, but I am okay now."

I laid a flower by his bed and said goodbye.

The next day, his wife called for my assistance in desperation, explaining that K.A. was in a cold sweat. I rushed to the hospital. When I arrived, he was completely soaked with a pulse of 180/minute and blood pressure of 60/40—close to shock. The nurse assured me that his wife made him nervous and was solely responsible for the stress. I insisted on seeing the director of surgery and threatened a lawsuit if he did not come in to take a look. Finally, he relented and agreed to re-examine his patient. He took him back into surgery and opened his chest, where he then removed two liters of blood. As it turned out, a couple of sutures had been poorly placed, causing his blood vessel to burst. He survived the second operation, but became blind in both eyes. On further close examination, it was discovered that the radiologist and the surgeon had completely misread the angiography. His coronary had not been narrowing at all. He later recovered his vision in one eye, but remains practically blind in the other.

These two cases show just a few examples of how the profit motive distorts our health care delivery system. In the first instance, the doctor was motivated by retaining a client, rather than treating his patient's condition. In the second, the physicians made a rash decision before verifying the test, as surgery proved to be the more profitable and immediate option.

Our for-profit health care system incentivizes physicians to prioritize the most lucrative forms of treatment over the quality of patient care. While insurance, hospitals, and pharmaceutical companies reap extra revenues, ultimately, these practices waste an estimated $1.5 trillion every year, or almost half of our nation's entire health care spending. We waste $700 billion on unnecessary tests and surgeries, $156 billion on fraudulent billing, $650 billion on administrative costs, and we pay $35.6 billion more for the same amount of pharmaceuticals relative to our Canadian neighbors.[2] [3] [4] [5] More troubling, the drive to maximize profits kills and maims several hundred thousand patients every year, who pay dearly for often unnecessary procedures and prescriptions.

Spending v. Waste, in Billions US$

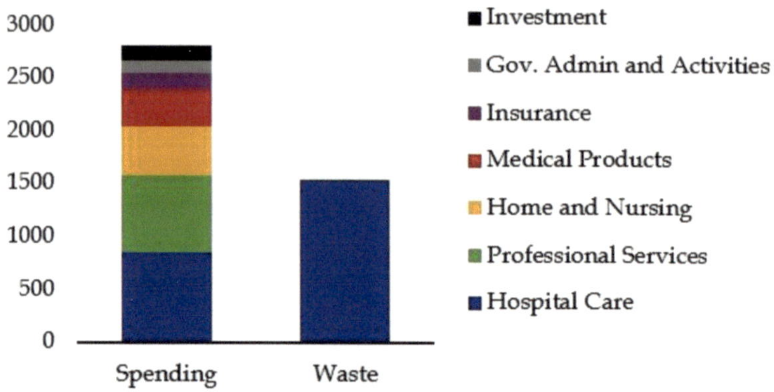

Source: Center for Medicare and Medicaid Services, National Health Expenditures data, 2012.

Waste Disected, in Billions US$

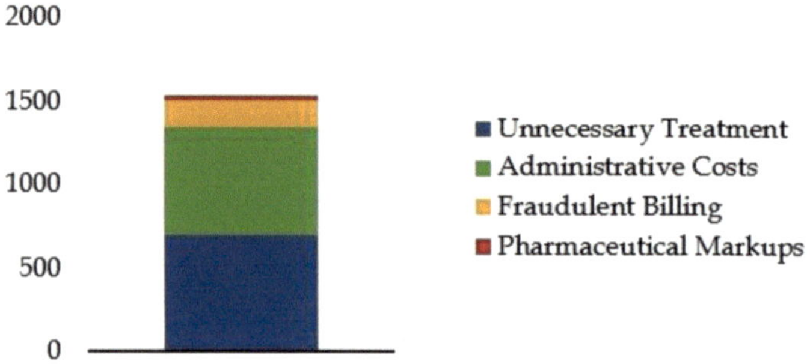

This book is not intended to demonize profit or the fundamental nature of our free market economy. Nor is it meant to attribute ill intention to any specific individuals or institutions. In most cases, profit is not necessarily bad, as it serves as the motivational force behind the creation of business and hence the expansion of our economy. Without profit, innovation throughout our economy would be undoubtedly stymied. However, in certain circumstances, the profit motive stands in opposition to improvements in efficiency, innovation, and quality.

In no other sector of our economy does the consumer have so much at stake. Not only must the clients pay for a service, but they are hedging their bodies at the same time. Paying for health care is not simply a monetary transaction, but rather an investment in one's life. Like any investment, it may pay dividends or incur losses depending on the quality of its results. From a financial perspective, the patient is both the client of a service and an investor in its success. To complicate matters, while the service itself may cost a specific amount of money, its outcome is difficult to measure.

Our health care system does not include, in its calculus, the true nature of the patient's investment. Rather, the system is distorted in favor of peripheral stakeholders, such as insurance companies, for-profit providers, and the pharmaceutical industry. These peripheral forces are motived by an interest to provide a product or service, rather than treat an ailment. They may indeed benefit financially by keeping us sick. As a result, their provisions do not always correspond with the most effective outcome for the patient. Because they have little stake in patient health, they invest their resources in a way that often inhibits quality, innovation, and efficiency. It is the interests of these parties, indifferent to the quality of care, which set improper incentives in our health care system. They are incentives that maximize the quantity of care over its quality.

Three main factors derived from the profit motive plague our current system. The industry responsible for our wellbeing is corrupted by 1) a professional conflict of interest between doctors, pharmaceutical companies, institutional research, and the patients they serve, 2) an asymmetry of information between doctors and patients, and 3) a lack of accountability across all sectors of the fragmented system. Simply put, the profit motive biases doctors towards the wrong practices and patients have no way to determine the right ones. Moreover, the mechanisms to punish malpractice lead to expensive and sometimes harmful practices of defensive medicine, while failing to address the depth of the real problem or provide patients with proper compensation.

In the following section, we explore the nature of the problem and set the stage for a comprehensive solution. While the deficiencies of our health care system have become complex, the solution is quite simple. Health care, as a sector of our economy, must be separated from the profit motive. This separation is both a moral and economic imperative. Doing so, however, does not require the cumbersome and politically toxic process of "socializing" the system to create a single-payer government-run plan. Instead, I advocate for a third way, one that establishes an independent nonprofit health care cooperative, controlled and monitored by the direct vote of the policy holders. This independent co-op will be a truly nonprofit corporation. With minimum bureaucracy and without the profit motive, my plan addresses the three main failings of the current system, while saving hundreds of billions of dollars to the benefit of the patient and the taxpayer.

Previous proposals to overhaul the health care industry have not addressed the root of the problem. Obama's Affordable Care Act (ACA), only prescribes a partial remedy—a bandaide on the insidious wound of our broken system. Though the ACA calls for the creation of a nonprofit insurance company to bring down prices for more Americans, it fails to capitalize on the need to reduce administrative waste and curb the exponential rise in health care costs. More importantly, it does not address the fundamental incentives that continue to distort the system in favor of the profit motivated pharmaceutical industry, insurance companies, and for-profit providers. As we prepare to implement an overhaul that may define the nature of our health care system for years to come, it is imperative that we confront these problems now.

Unintended Genocide

> *If a physician make a large incision with the operating knife, and kill him, or open a tumor with the operating knife, and cut out the eye, his hands shall be cut off.*
>
> – *Hammurabi's Code of Laws*, no. 218.[6]

THE ABOVE EXCERPT FROM HAMMURABI'S CODE OF LAWS represents the first malpractice law ever written. Today, nearly 4,000 years later, instances of malpractice do not warrant punishments like 'an eye for an eye,' or in this case, 'hands for an eye.' However, the severity of potential mistakes made during surgical procedures is enough to make many doctors conceal malpractice from the public.

Hidden within our national death statistics is a fatal epidemic, known as iatrogenesis, which refers to illness, injury or death caused by medical practitioners. Of the 2.5 million deaths that occur in the US every year, an estimated 797,926 (32 percent) are caused by improper hospital care or mistakes made by doctors and hospital staff.[7] In other words, 2,164 Americans die every day just by seeking medical care. Even this staggering number may be too low, as it is estimated that only one quarter of cases are ever reported. While natural human error is to blame for much of the tragedy, this incredible loss of life is fueled in part, by a drive to perform profitable, yet often unnecessary, treatments. As a physician, with over 40 years of experience within our health care system, I was well aware of iatrogenic illness and even death, but had no idea of the extent of the tragedy.

Every year, 16.4 million people undergo completely unnecessary medical events, including 8.9 million unnecessary hospitalizations and 7.5 million unnecessary procedures. Of the total, 3.08 million cause harm to the patient. With an average fatality rate of 14 percent for iatrogenic complications, it is estimated that 431,200 people die every year, as a direct result of completely unnecessary medical events.[8] Over the last 12 years, our for-profit health care system has essentially killed the equivalent of the more than five million Jews that perished in the Holocaust. Quite shockingly, Hitler's Third Reich terrorized Europe for the same number years.

We are witness to a silent and unintended genocide. Unlike the highly publicized atrocities of the early 20th century perpetrated in the name of eugenics, the iatrogenic catastrophe of the 21st century remains out of sight. Our nation's annual mortality report, published by the Centers for Disease Control (CDC), makes no mention of medical error as a cause of death. Yet in reality, the number of iatrogenic deaths surpasses the highest reported cause of death: heart disease. In the medical profession, there exists a culture of infallibility, a sense that doctors do not make mistakes. If they do, they shield each other, protected from the wrath of the public. As a result, when errors do occur they are most often denied. Many studies estimate that only 5 to 25 percent of malpractice is ever reported.[9] The vast majority of reporting comes from patients and their family members alone.

Over forty years as a physician, I have witnessed countless medical mistakes and cover-ups. One instance during my residency at the Mallory Institute of Pathology—one of our nation's oldest and most prestigious institutes of pathology, affiliated with Harvard, Tufts, and Boston University—gives a glimpse into the extent of the problem.

I remember performing an autopsy on a patient who had died with an abdomen full of blood. The man had suffered from 20 years of chronic lymphocytic leukemia, which had caused his spleen to become enlarged. However, the extent of bleeding did not seem consistent with the man's chronic illness. So I stayed late that night, examining every inch of the cadaver. When I first looked at the spleen, everything appeared to match the patient's chronic condition. But, upon closer examination, I noticed something different. A tiny hole, the size of a large needle point could be found on one side of the spleen. After examining the deceased's hospital records, I saw that he had undergone a needle biopsy of the liver, which confirmed that the man's fatal internal bleeding had been the result of an accidental spleen puncture during the biopsy procedure.

Having finished the examination, I drafted a new autopsy report stating the man's cause of death to be bleeding from a punctured spleen caused by the liver biopsy. I passed it on to my supervisor. As he read my conclusions, I noticed his look of disapproval.

"You can't write this," he said.

"Why not?" I asked.

"Because the man clearly died of chronic lymphocytic leukemia," he said, gesturing for me to sign a different report stating that the patient had died of his own health condition. Defiant, I refused to sign my name on the report.

A week later, Professor George Kenneth Mallory, the head of the institute and son of its founder, called me into his office. He asked me why I had refused to sign off on the autopsy and I explained to him my findings on the patient's cause of death. He paused for a second and looked concerned.

"You could write the cause of death as chronic lymphocytic leukemia and add puncture of the spleen as an incidental finding," he said.

"But sir, the man had leukemia for 20 years, yet died abruptly of bleeding from a punctured spleen," reiterating that I would not sign a false report.

He seemed upset, but still determined to resolve the problem.

"Give me the file," he said, looking me straight in the eye. With a stroke, he signed the document and dismissed me from his office. One of the nation's most highly respected pathologists had just covered up a fatal medical error. I never brought attention to this particular case again and was surprised that he never fired me. I could only imagine the many cover ups that never even made it to his desk.

Since 2002, projections indicate that 164 million Americans or 56 percent of the population has received unnecessary medical care. With so many unnecessary surgeries, we increase the likelihood of medical error. Not only are there more opportunities to make a mistake, but the increased patient load limits the amount of time physicians are able to spend on each patient.

The profit motive alone is directly responsible for over half of all fatalities caused by medical error. Yet, economics only tell part of the story of our dysfunctional health care system. The rest can be found in the loss of life and physical suffering of patients, and the pain felt by their friends and families.

How Doctors Became Beholden to Profit, Not Patients

BEFORE WE VENTURE TO UNDERSTAND THE FAILINGS OF OUR current health care system, it is important to know how it began. While we currently spend one sixth of our GDP on health care, back in 1960 we paid just 5 percent. The majority of this rise occurred from 1980 to 1990, a decade of various government reforms permitting for-profit practices in the health care industry.

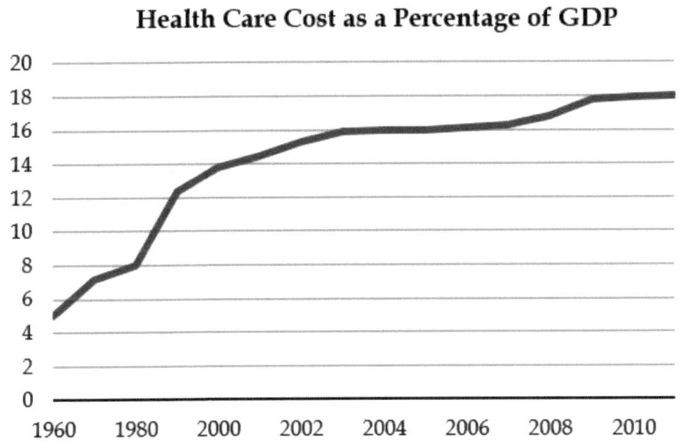

The traditional US health care system used a pay-for-service model, with self-employed doctors answerable directly to their patients.[10] Patients chose their physician, who often knew them personally and usually paid for the care directly. If patients did not like the price of care or found it ineffective, they were free to choose another doctor. Doctors had a strong incentive to please their patients.[11] Their financial security and community standing depended on it.

In his book, *The Profit Motive and Patient Care*, Bradford H. Gray describes a rich history of independence among physicians. "Self-employment, fee-for-service payment, and a passive orientation on the part of third party payers...were integral to the profession's concept of the ideal doctor-patient relationship." He notes, "[a] considerable degree of autonomy has long characterized medical practice in the Unites States," and "[a] decline in physician autonomy denotes much more than a major change in the occupation." He explains this erosion of independence, as the downfall of the doctor-patient relationship.[12]

Between 1960 and 1980, the number of medical school graduates doubled largely due to new federal funding for education.[13] The influx in medical professionals had a profound impact on health care provision. In 1978, there was one physician for every 584 people in the United States.[14] Today, there is one physician per 375 people. With a shrinking patient base, over time, the medical profession became increasingly competitive and commercialized. Competition to earn the same income on fewer patients, led to extensive overutilization and over-billing for services. Doctors and hospitals were paid by faceless third-parties from private insurance and government. Patients received a copy of the bill detailing the charges, but since they weren't paying, they simply forgot about it. The paying party did not know what it was being billed for and the service recipient had nothing to say about it.

Meanwhile, government reforms meant to expand coverage, merely allowed emerging for-profit entities to exploit the system in their favor. Dr. Ezekiel J. Emanuel, the author of *Healthcare Guaranteed* and brother of former White House Chief of Staff Rahm Emanuel, aptly describes the nature of past reform. "Since the passage of Medicare and Medicaid in 1965, healthcare reformers have in effect focused on rearranging the chairs on the Titanic, enacting cosmetic changes that ignore the system's true failures." Our government has used a piecemeal approach to control costs, while in fact allowing the for-profit health care industry to take advantage of extra government dollars.[15]

To meet the needs of a growing number of Medicare recipients, in the 1980s, legislation enabled the private sector to develop for-profit, investor-owned hospitals and later health maintenance organizations (HMOs). The new laws also permitted these for-profit providers to market and advertise their medical services.[16] Previously, doctors were only allowed to put their name, specialty, office address, and phone number in their community yellow pages. The entire industry considered advertising unprofessional and patients only sought help when they needed it. During the same decade, hospitals, HMOs, pharmaceuticals, and insurance companies began to advertise their products and services, giving them an advantage over independent doctors and smaller practices. In order to attract patients, doctors had to either join these companies or contract with their services and payment plans. On the face of it, patients became tools of profit. Instead of allowing patients the freedom to choose the right doctor and hospital, physicians and hospitals were forced to actively clamor for customers through for-profit third-party contracts.

Many patient-dependent practices became organization-dependent practices, as the cost of health insurance sky-rocketed and many patients opted to switch to health care provider networks, like HMOs.[17] Many doctors who contracted with these corporate health providers were no longer answerable to their patients for treatment decisions, but rather to the organizations that attracted their patient base. A gap widened between doctors and their patients, filled by third-party, for-profit enterprises. The reality of patient health needs gradually faded into the background. If hospital beds were empty, doctors were incentivized to prolong their patient's stay; if others were waiting, the patient was sent home, ready or not. Doctors, dependent on organizations for their professional income, no longer had the power to make medical decisions for medical reasons alone; economics became a deciding factor.

When profit focused corporations seized the pay-for-service model, doctors had to provide more health care than necessary or risk a massive drop in pay. Since HMOs also took a "cut" of the health care business, doctors earned less per patient than in private practice and were forced to diversify their income with medical entrepreneurship.

At first, doctors could bill for all procedures, which allowed them to earn a little extra income. But eventually, third-party payers began to insist that the providers bill them exclusively. To supplement their income, doctors had to provide additional and often unnecessary services or invest directly in laboratories and other facilities to where they referred patients.[18] These practices eventually comprised a significant portion of their medical income. To keep up with the rate of overutilization, hospitals and testing facilities began operating at near or full capacity.

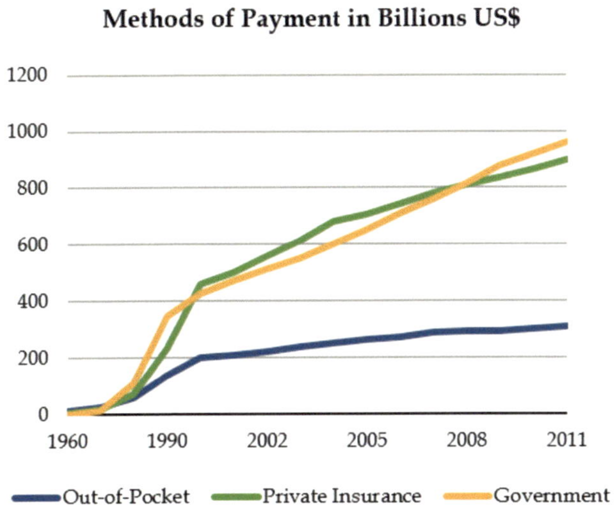

Nevertheless, the increased cost remained invisible to individual patients. Most costs were covered by private health insurance or Medicare. Doctors and hospitals often waived the co-payment paid by patients to keep them coming in for services. Since the patients did not pay directly, this practice encouraged over-utilization. Insurance companies and health providers accrued profits through gradual increases to insurance premiums and billing the government. Unbeknownst to the patients, this practice slowly escalated the cost of medical care. Since most patients no longer paid directly for their care, they became unable to hold their doctors accountable for ineffective treatment. Moreover, they also lacked the information and experience to identify unnecessary tests, drugs, and procedures. The intense asymmetry of information between the providers and receivers of health care, came to favor corporate interests over the best intention of doctors.

In the medical economy that arose, large for-profit competitors jockeyed for a limited number of patients, and doctors found themselves having to run competitive businesses with mounting administrative costs. Physicians had to balance the interests of many players, against the interests of the patients. By this point, the old model of the doctor-patient relationship had completely broken down. As doctors were forced to make compromises on their treatment decisions, public attitudes about the medical profession began to change. The trust that people had once felt for their doctors in the 1960s was replaced by a deep skepticism.[19]

Health and Profit: A Deep Conflict

PROFIT FORCES OUR HEALTH CARE PROVIDERS TO PLAY THE part of businessperson, under the guise of caregiver. In some cases, it incentivizes doctors to overprescribe tests and treatments, in others it encourages them to do too little. It encourages the pharmaceutical industry to direct its money towards biased medical education and places profit-driven industry advertising where impartial information should be. It corrupts congressmen with connections to the for-profit health care industry to influence FDA officials to approve devices and drugs that often harm people or are largely ineffective.

It takes a strongly ethical person to put the interest of the patient before his or her own financial interests. The conflict of interests endemic to for-profit health care does not mean that all providers are intrinsically corrupt, or morally questionable. In reality, the system itself makes it difficult for even well-intentioned health care providers to prioritize the patient.

The current payment structures in oncology encourage doctors and hospitals to treat cancer indefinitely with chemotherapy, rather than attempt curative or preventative alternatives. Medicare pays for 80 percent of oncology bills and the other 20 percent is paid by secondary insurance, Medicaid, Medicare, or forgiven. The longer doctors extend treatment, the more they are able to charge Medicare. Much of the money generated by chemotherapy is pure profit. In 2005, Medicare attempted to limit the profit made by private practice oncologists by adjusting the reimbursement rate for certain drugs related to cancer. That year, oncologists billed $1 billion less than the previous year. One oncologist, Dr. Robert Geller, described the situation this way, "[p]eople go where the money is, and you'd like to believe it's different in medicine, but it's really no different in medicine. When you start thinking of oncology as a business, then all these decisions make sense."[20] Whatever their best intentions, doctors are not always incentivized to cure cancer, but instead to treat it indefinitely.

We find a clear example in the treatment of recurrent prostate cancer. Oncologists generally treat recurrent prostate cancer through a number of phases. They begin first with radiation and wait and see if the cancer recurs, then they treat it with hormonal therapy by reducing the patient's testosterone; they then follow it up with chemotherapy, and finally immunotherapy. Oncologists are generally reluctant to combine these treatments to maximize the additive therapeutic effect. Prolonging treatment is extremely profitable, but wastes a tremendous amount of money and causes years of suffering, often at limited improvements to the patient's quality of life. Rather than cure the ailment once and for all, the logic of profit motivated cancer therapy, treats the symptoms without ever fully eliminating the cause, thereby ensuring a lifelong customer.

Doctors themselves suffer from having to manage the conflicting goals of running for-profit practices and providing patient care. Recent years have seen a dramatic increase in the number of doctors suffering from symptoms of "physician burnout." In a recent study, 46 percent of physicians reported chronic fatigue, unprofessional behavior, lack of empathy, anger, irritation, impatience, and lack of interest.[21] Physicians are stretched too thin. The suicide rate for physicians is much higher than other professions—about 40 percent higher for men, and 130 percent higher for women.[22] From treating patients properly to managing an effective business, our physicians have become overloaded by administrative duties that extend beyond their professional training. The result creates a massive opportunity cost in which physicians end up dedicating less of their energy towards diagnosis and treatment and more towards paper work and business management. For the physician, the stress may lead to substance abuse, depression, and family problems. For patients, it may mean a missed diagnosis or ineffective care.

In its many forms, our for-profit health care system does not work in the interest of the patient or our society at large. In the pay-for-service model, doctors have the incentive to overprescribe costly and often dangerous procedures and medication. In the health maintenance organization (HMO) model, doctors are encouraged to be "efficient" with treatment in a way that underserves the patient. Other important structures include the independent practice association (IPA) and the preferred provider organization (PPO). The PPO functions through the pay-for-service-model and encourages over-utilization on a massive scale. The IPA combines the problems of under and over utilization through a series of different arrangements. In nearly every case, the profit motive fails to properly address the needs of patients and creates several hundred billion dollars in waste, not to mention extensive human suffering and death.

Overutilization: The Pay-for-Service Model

Let us put some human faces to the consequences of the profit motivated, pay-for-service model. Madeline was a generally healthy 71-year-old woman who had just retired after 30 years of hard work. She had surgery to remove a tumor in the right side of her abdomen. The surgery was successful, but during the operation the doctor made an accidental incision in her small intestine. Following the procedure, her bowel movements stopped for a time. A non-invasive, wait-and-see approach is usually recommended in this situation. Instead of watchful waiting, her doctor rushed her into emergency exploratory surgery, and removed approximately 13 feet of her small intestine. This surgery led to an infection and a third surgery that removed even more of her small intestine. Fourth and fifth surgeries removed more and more. Following the first unnecessary surgery, Madeline suffered through five additional surgeries, 11 months of hospitalization, and must be fed through a tube for the rest of her life. To make matters worse, tube feeding, which takes 12 hours each day, has required repeated procedures to replace the tube and treat its subsequent infections. Madeline suffers from constant diarrhea, fatigue, nausea, and bloating, which severely limit her daily activities. Unnecessary surgeries served to enrich the surgeon and hospital, at the cost of Madeline's freedom to enjoy the retirement she worked so hard to achieve. She will be fed from a tube for the rest of her life.[23]

Madeline's story cannot be solved by placing blame on any one doctor, even if that doctor did, in fact make mistakes. Rather, her story is indicative of a larger issue: an incentive structure that prioritizes patient fees above patient care.

In the pay-for-service model, profit incentivizes doctors to prescribe too much care, often harming patients and raising insurance rates. Most US government programs and private insurance policies employ the "pay-for-service" model of health care delivery. Under this model, every prescription and treatment makes money for the provider organization. But frequently, the medical practices of physicians intertwine with their financial stakes in the pharmaceutical and insurance industries. Many doctors own shares in the hospitals, biotech companies, pharmaceutical companies, and device companies to which they refer patients. Some doctors collect consultant fees from these corporations or sit on their boards of directors. As a result, "pay-for-service" incentivizes physicians to recommend more treatment and act on their financial bias for particular devices, medications, and surgeries.

Unnecessary treatment has become rampant in our for-profit "pay-for-service" system. Sixty percent of surgeries performed every year are unnecessary.[24] In his book, *Death by Medicine*, Gary Null estimates that American physicians perform 7.5 million unnecessary surgeries each year.[25] In total, we spend over $700 billion on completely unnecessary tests, hospitalizations, and procedures. According to an estimate by Peter Orszag, Former Director of the Congressional Budget Office, about 5 percent of the nation's entire GDP is wasted on tests and procedures that offer no medical benefit.[26] Among the medical specialties, interventional cardiology and gastroenterology have the highest rates of overutilization. People with heartburn symptoms are given an endoscopy before other diagnostic tests, perhaps because endoscopies earn doctors between $600 and $1,200. Other examples of overutilization include follow-up colonoscopies, which doctors frequently order more than once every five years, even though that level of vigilance is neither necessary nor useful. For chest pain and other symptoms, doctors prescribe angioplasty with stent placement, despite evidence suggesting that such procedures do not help patients and may even cause harm.[27] The United States leads the world in interventional cardiology surgery, but does not boast better survival rates to show for it.[28]

Consider the case of McAllen, Texas, where a profit-based incentive structure has led to systematic over-billing. In McAllen, the Medicare program pays an average of $15,000 per person per year, around double the national per capita cost of Medicare.[29] And yet, the average person in McAllen makes an annual income of just $12,000. In other words, the government is paying for a health policy worth a quarter more than the recipient's earnings.

But, why does health care in McAllen cost so much? Studies have shown that the people of McAllen are no healthier than typical Americans. Furthermore, no evidence suggests that McAllen hospitals provide better quality care. Several studies conducted by economists at Dartmouth University shed some light on the true reasons behind the high cost of care. Their research indicates that "those in higher-spending regions are more likely to be admitted to the hospital, spend more time in the hospital, receive more discretionary tests, see more medical specialists, and have many more different physicians involved in their care." However, "the extra care does not produce better outcomes overall or result in better quality of care."[30]

The same Dartmouth studies revealed that health care in McAllen suffers from rampant overutilization. According to Medicare data, from 2001 to 2005, McAllen patients received 50 percent more specialist visits than patients in El Paso. Between 2005 and 2006, they received 30 percent more bone-density studies, 60 percent more stress tests with echocardiography, 200 percent more nerve-conduction studies to diagnose carpal-tunnel syndrome, and 550 percent more urine-flow studies to diagnose prostate troubles. The list goes on. One medical student reported a case in which a McAllen doctor ordered a colonoscopy—a preventive procedure—for a terminally ill patient. Although the doctor and the hospital earned a bit of extra revenue from the referral, the test served no medical purpose.[31]

Physicians in McAllen are paid on a fee-for-service basis, and at the local Renaissance Hospital, they also receive a portion of company profits, which in 2007 totaled $34 million. Many of the private doctors in McAllen hold financial stakes in local for-profit hospitals, laboratories, and testing facilities. They refer patients to these hospitals, in exchange for annual payments ranging from $100,000 to $500,000 per doctor, per year.[32]

Contrast this arrangement with the incentive structure at the Mayo Clinic in Rochester, Minnesota. The Mayo Clinic in Minnesota boasts Medicare costs of $6,688 per person, significantly below the national average of $8,680.[33] The main difference between McAllen and the Mayo Clinic is that Mayo Clinic doctors are paid on a salary rather than by the gross number of surgeries, treatments, and tests that they perform. Because doctors are salaried, there is absolutely no incentive to overprescribe. As a result, they spend more time with patients and administer fewer tests, procedures, and medications. The Mayo Clinic's quality-of-care rankings continue to make the top of the list.[34]

Unnecessary surgeries and procedures endanger patients. Experts estimated that 90 percent of the 750,000 hysterectomies performed each year are unnecessary, making the hysterectomy one of the most common unnecessary surgeries after coronary bypass.[35] Physicians should not perform hysterectomies until all other options have been exhausted. However, the profit motive incentivizes physicians to perform as many hysterectomies as possible.[36] Women suffer terribly from this serious procedure, particularly when ovaries are removed. In addition to sudden menopause, the surgery causes between 16 and 57 percent of women to lose ovarian function prematurely, which in turn contributes to rapid loss of bone density and osteoporosis. Every year, 2,500 women die from the procedure.[37]

Heart surgery is the most common unnecessary surgical procedure in America. In 2002, insurers paid hospitals an average of $29,300 for each coronary bypass surgery, with $6,800 in net profit, per surgery earned by for-profit health providers.[38] A study by CardioQual, found that 43 percent of the angioplasties investigated were unnecessary and "outside reasonable expected medical practice." Between 1998 and 2001, researchers discovered that the United States performed twice as many angioplasties per capita as other developed nations, but saw the same health outcomes.[39] Patients over 80 years old received heart surgery at an especially high rate, but their mortality was identical to those of the same age in Canada who did not undergo surgery. Dr. Thomas Riles, the chief of surgery at New York University's Medical Center, captured the nature of overuse from a global perspective: "recently, I lectured in Korea and Japan. And over there, they do a fraction of the surgeries we do—perhaps 10 percent. I would say they do too few, but we're at the other end of the spectrum. We do too many."

Many coronary bypass surgeries do not help the patient and may cause serious side effects, including stroke, brain damage, memory loss, kidney failure, heart attack, internal bleeding, heartbeat irregularity, and chest infection.[40] Because coronary bypass surgery is so dangerous, it should be performed sparingly. However, an entire industry worth millions of dollars to surgeons and medical device patent holders has transformed heart surgery it into common practice.

Underutilization: The False Nonprofit Model

Current attempts to manage the entire process of providing health care fail to do so effectively. Unlike the pay-for-service model, which over-prescribes unnecessary procedures, health maintenance organizations (HMOs), like Kaiser are incentivized to provide insufficient care. An HMO pays its doctors on a salary basis and contracts with hospitals and clinics to provide services. Patients who contract with an HMO must stay within the organization's network. In addition, patients must choose a primary care physician who is responsible for making decisions on behalf of the patient regarding referrals, surgery, and other procedures. As compared with PPOs and IPAs, which we will discuss shortly, HMOs tend to offer patients lower prices, but with more restrictions on choice.

In name, Kaiser claims to be nonprofit and structured to serve patients. In practice, Kaiser consists of a nonprofit branch and a for-profit branch, with porous boundaries that enable the transfer of money between both segments of the business.[41] Kaiser has three divisions. Two of them—the Kaiser Foundation Health Plan and Kaiser Foundation Hospitals—are nonprofit. The third division, Permanente Medical Groups is for-profit. This latter organization is made up of Kaiser physician partners, who after working a certain number of years, have been selected by existing group members to share in Kaiser's revenue. After covering costs and paying salaries, Kaiser pays partner physicians bonuses using leftover revenue not spent on treating patients. Unlike doctors in pay-for-service plans, who are incentivized to provide unnecessary treatment, Kaiser physicians are incentivized to skimp on care for its 8.9 million policy holders.[42]

This keeps the insurance premiums competitive for employers who buy their employees health care, while funneling profit to the partners of Permanente Medical Group. The partners of Kaiser Medical Groups receive electronic report cards on all salaried doctors, listing their total expenditures on care. The more care physicians provide, the less money the partner physicians receive at the end of the year. If doctors seek to join the ranks of the privileged partners, they must first show "efficiency" in the care they provide. Salaried doctors know that to remain in the good graces of the partners and have a chance at eventually joining their ranks, they must demonstrate that they do not prescribe too much, test too much, or treat too much. They must show they are cost effective doctors, particularly with expensive treatments. The pressure Kaiser places on its staff to be "efficient" creates a contentious incentive structure that can leads to a substandard quality of care.

Kaiser will often avoid expensive checkups in the interest of cost efficiency, but at a serious risk to the patient. An acquaintance of mine had been a member of Kaiser for years. At age 62, he began to worry about the risk of colon cancer, as his father died of the affliction at 55. Over the course of five years, he asked several of his Kaiser physicians for a colonoscopy, a procedure absolutely necessary to catch this form of cancer in its early stages. However, each time, his physicians reassured him that it was not necessary. He became increasingly concerned when he noticed his stomach was expanding. Finally, he took a photo of his bloated belly to show the doctor. He demanded action and was eventually given a colonoscopy. The examination revealed that he had an aggressive form of colon cancer, which had already spread to the liver. By this point, the cancer had become terminal and he died shortly after the diagnosis. Had he undergone a routine colonoscopy three years earlier, he would have most likely survived.

The Middlemen

Besides HMOs, several other arrangements help coordinate massive patient networks. Preferred provider organizations (PPOs) are similar to HMOs, but with several important differences. PPOs and HMOs are both networks of health care providers that leverage their size to make bulk purchases on physician services and medical products. However, PPOs act as middlemen, not as managers, coordinating the flow of patients to private practices, rather than running the hospitals, clinics, and employing the doctors themselves. In general, PPOs offer patients more choice than HMOs, as well as more responsibility, but at a higher cost. Patients in a PPO may choose their physicians from a larger network, can select from outside the network, have a wider variety of treatment options, and are not required to select a primary care physician. However, premiums tend to be higher under PPO contracts, such as Blue Shield and Blue Cross, than HMO contracts.

PPOs consist of a series of contracts between participating providers and a third-party insurance company. Eighty-seven percent of doctors have at least one of these kinds of "managed care" contracts covering some of their patients.[43] PPOs require doctors within their networks to charge discounted rates for treating patients referred to them. The PPO contracts with the insurance company by charging an access fee, in exchange for sending patients to doctors included in the PPO network. The physicians provide services and the PPO acts as the middleman, taking a percentage of revenue from the transaction. Most physicians rely on PPOs to maintain a steady stream of patients. However, because they are paid less for each service, physicians are incentivized to provide more services for the same medical conditions.

Independent practice associations (IPAs) create the worst incentive structure, combining the problems of overutilization with those of underutilization. IPAs function similar to PPOs, but they contract with HMOs rather than insurance companies. IPAs are organizations comprised of physicians who maintain their independent practices, but join together under the IPA banner in order to leverage greater negotiating power. IPAs act as contracting agencies. Under the IPA, doctors are either paid under a set pay-for-service fee or one large monthly fee for the number of patients covered: an incentive structure known as "capitation."

Capitation encourages doctors to provide minimal care to as many patients as possible to meet the obligation under the capitation contract.[44] If doctors spend time caring for "capitation" patients, they proportionately lose time that otherwise would be available for taking on additional pay-for-service patients. For example, if a doctor receives $10,000 per month in exchange for covering a maximum of 1,000 patients under "capitation," the doctor only makes $100 on each patient. As a result, he or she is incentivized to cut corners and spend half the time, or about five minutes, on each "capitation" patient. The doctor's natural tendency is to skimp on "capitation" patients, for the sake of more lucrative fee-for-service patients. Consequently, because the doctor has less time, he or she is also encouraged to overprescribe for fee-for-service treatments in order to make up the difference. HMOs use the IPA model to save money by negotiating bulk capitation with doctors, effectively cutting the cost required to provide for each patient.[45]

Biased Information

Corporate interests corrupt the material taught in medical school, creating biased health care information. The federal government funds certain types of medical education, but corporations also contribute a significant portion of the funding. This practice affects the perception among doctors of what medical information counts as scientific and objective. Often this educational material is based on made-to-order research funded by the marketing budgets of pharmaceutical companies. The source of funding has a profound effect on medical information.

Lacking reliable information, doctors cannot provide effective care.

Today, the Department of Health and Human Services (HHS) is the largest funder of graduate medical education (GME), paying about $9.5 billion in Medicare funds and $2 billion in Medicaid dollars each year to train new doctors. Every year, 115,000 medical school graduates in residency programs learn to practice medicine in more than 1,000 teaching hospitals. Federal funding for each resident amounts to $100,000 a year.[46]

Before Medicare was established in 1965, hospitals funded the majority of GME. After Medicare, the federal government became the primary funder of GME. Initially, legislators believed that another source would eventually replace Medicare, but so far this has not happened. Today, Medicare and Medicaid constitute 83 percent of federal spending on GME. Other government funding streams include, the US Department of Veterans Affairs (10 percent), the Department of Defense (3 percent), and the Bureau of Health Professions (3 percent). GME is considered a "public good" and receives billions from state and federal public funds.[47]

The rest of GME is paid for by private insurers. Because of the nature of GME accounting, it has proved difficult to track how much money flows into GME from these sources. Contracts are numerous, highly variable, and are not centrally tracked. As a result, there are no national figures that fully account for GME funding from these sources.[48]

On the other hand, we do know that the pharmaceutical industry funds about 45 percent of continuing medical education (CME). All practicing doctors covering patients under Medicare and Medicaid are required to periodically enroll in continuing medical education, in order to keep their licenses. In 2011, total funding for CME was $2.3 billion. Of that amount, the pharmaceutical industry provided $736 million in grants and $296 million in advertising revenue. Pharmaceutical companies pay CME providers to place advertisements in medical meeting exhibit halls. Registration fees paid by doctors out-of-pocket accounted for the remaining $1.2 billion. In 2006, industry dollars as a portion of CME funding reached an all-time high of 50 percent [49].[49]

Year	Total CME Funding	Industry Support	Ad & Exhibit Revenue	Registration Fees & Other Revenue
2006	$2.38 billion	$1.19 billion	$245 million	$940 million
2007	$2.54 billion	$1.21 billion	$274 million	$1.05 billion
2008	$2.37 billion	$1.04 billion	$277 million	$1.05 billion
2009	$2.18 billion	$856 million	$283 million	$1.05 billion
2010	$2.24 billion	$831 million	$277 million	$1.13 billion
2011	$2.3 billion	$736 million	$296 million	$1.2 billion

CME funding sources, 2006-2010.[50]

One expert estimates that pharmaceutical companies spend $35 billion each year towards influencing medical education. It is very difficult to say exactly how much, because pharmaceutical companies keep these figures secret, and disguise the money spent towards medical education by presenting it as marketing costs. In 2001, when the pharmaceutical industry disclosed that it spent $19 billion on marketing, it also left another $35 billion in the marketing budget completely unaccounted for. Marcia Angell, the former editor-in-chief of the *New England Journal of Medicine*, writes about the pharmaceutical industry's payments towards educational activities: "although no outsider knows for sure, they [education activities] probably account for the lion's share of the missing $35 billion of the marketing budget."

In the classroom, the pharmaceutical industry often presents a false image of the best treatments. One Harvard student, Matt Zerden, became apprehensive during his first-year pharmacology class when he noticed his professor's unusual enthusiasm for promoting certain drugs for lowering cholesterol. Zerden grew more alarmed when the professor dismissively brushed aside one student's question about side effects. Zerden went online and was shocked to discover that ten pharmaceutical companies were paying his professor as a consultant and five of those companies sold drugs that he recommended to purportedly lower cholesterol.[51]

Soon afterward, the American Medical Student Association, a national watchdog group devoted to monitoring and limiting the use and abuse of pharmaceutical industry money, gave Harvard an "F" when it came to separating drug industry influence from medical education. Zerden voiced his concerns to his peers, and over the next four years, more than 200 Harvard Medical students and faculty members joined together to protest the university's submission to the influence of the pharmaceutical industry.

The current dean of Harvard Medical School, Dr. Jeffrey S. Flier, once received a $500,000 research grant from Bristol-Myers Squibb and served as a consultant for several Cambridge biotechnology companies.[52] Once this information became public, Dr. Flier claimed to break all ties to the industry. Nevertheless, he failed to mention his continued co-chairmanship at Alinea Pharmaceuticals, his membership at Cantata Laboratories, and his numerous other intimate positions in the for-profit pharmaceutical industry.[53]

About 18 percent of the Harvard faculty admit that they or their family members have financial interests that conflict with their academic duties. One Harvard professor disclosed 47 individual connections to the pharmaceutical industry. Dr. Joseph B. Martin, Dean Emeritus of Harvard Medical School, received $197,000 each year for serving on the boards of two pharmaceutical corporations.[54]

The pharmaceutical industry spends billions to influence medical research. Pharmaceutical and biotech companies now fund more than 60 percent of all clinical studies in the United States.[55] The Bayh-Dole Act, passed in 1980, permitted universities to commercialize their products without losing federal research funding. In 1984, the pharmaceutical industry paid university researchers $26 million. By 2000, pharmaceutical industry contributions to university research had climbed to $2.3 billion, a ninety-fold increase.[56]

To demonstrate a case and point, Dr. Charles B. Nemeroff, a psychiatry professor at Atlanta's Emory University, wrote an article in *Nature Neuroscience* in which he made recommendations on the best psychiatric drugs. However, he did not disclose his direct financial stake in three of the treatments he deemed most effective, or his ownership of a personal patent on a transdermal patch used to dispense one of the medications. When other scientists asked *Nature Neuroscience* to publish a criticism of Nemeroff, the journal refused. The whistleblowers then took their article to the *New York Times*, which finally agreed to publish their findings. The article revealed that from

2000 to 2007, Nemeroff received more than $2.8 million in consulting arrangements, $1.2 million of which he failed to report.[57] After the story broke, some professional medical journals started to insist that all writers disclose their financial conflicts of interest, as they relate to the content of their articles. However, some journals still do not require these disclosures, and for those that do, enforcement is often lacking.[58]

Pharmaceutical industry influence on medical education is widespread. Several highly respected professors have made headlines for their explicit ties to pharmaceutical companies. While serving as the dean of University of Minnesota Medical School, Deborah E. Powel took a paid position with Pepsi in 2006.[59] A congressional investigation recently revealed that unnamed faculty members at Columbia and New York University had ghostwritten promotional industry articles.[60] Dr. Laurie Glimcher, Dean of Weill Cornell Medical College, maintains extensive corporate obligations. In 2010, Bristol-Myers Squibb awarded Glimcher with $244,500 in cash and $1.4 million in deferred share units.[61]

Studies funded by corporate interests are significantly more likely to report positive results, than studies funded by nonprofits without similar financial ties.[62] One study, conducted by Professor Francis C. Biley of Bournemouth University, indicated that pharmaceutical industry-funded publications on drugs makes it 90 percent certain that the drug will be perceived as useful. By contrast, impartial studies present favorable conclusions, only 50 percent of the time.[63] A Yale University study, published in the *Journal of the American Medical Association* (JAMA), revealed that researchers who publish unbiased negative results about drug, tend to have their funding penalized.

Researchers have openly admitted to delaying articles and changing results to benefit those paying for the studies.[64]

Pharmaceutical companies frequently pay medical researchers and physicians to sign their names on pseudo-research penned by industry PR departments. These subtle advertisements are presented as scientific information. Though estimating the exact frequency of ghostwriting is difficult, the practice is known to be widespread and effective. According to the *New York Times*, "placing such papers in medical journals has become a fundamental marketing practice for most of the large pharmaceutical companies."[65] Doctors frequently write articles for drug companies, which publish the articles in medical journals alongside scientific research. These ghostwriters remain anonymous.

The drug company Wyeth hired DesignWrite, a medical writing company, to prepare an estimated 60 articles favorable to Wyeth's hormone drugs, Premarin and Prempro.[66] Those articles had a clearly stated objective of making the drugs appear better and promoting their sale in medical journals. DesignWrite wrote that the goal of one article, for instance, was to de-emphasize the risk of breast cancer, promote the drug as a cure, and downplay the effectiveness of competing drugs. The DesignWrite articles were published in medical journals between 1998 and 2005. In 2002, researchers discovered that women who took Wyeth's hormone drugs actually suffered increased rates of breast cancer and heart disease. Doctors who prescribed the drug simply did not know any better, because the articles had been published alongside objective scientific research. The border between medical education and marketing has dissolved.

Pharmaceutical companies and device manufacturers often censor negative results from publication in medical journals. Negative result suppression often makes it to the highest level of the FDA.[67]

In 2004, Dr. Lazar Greenfield and Dr. Dale Tavris, two officials at the FDA wrote a paper titled "Aneurysm-Related Mortality Rates in the US AneuRx Clinical Trial," set to be published in the *Journal of Vascular Surgery*. AneuRx is a stent graft, a 5-inch metal and fabric cylinder. When a person suffers an aortic aneurysm, a bulge can develop on the main artery carrying blood away from the heart. The insertion of a stent is intended to allow blood to flow through the stent at the area of the bulge, relieving pressure on the artery and preventing it from rupturing.[68]

The FDA article criticized AneuRx. It argued that for certain patients, a different surgical procedure was less dangerous, even if it were more invasive. The alternative procedure advocated in the article, involved surgery and the insertion of a synthetic-fabric tube. Evidence suggested that while the synthetic-fabric tube caused fewer problems over time, the surgery involved in its installation was much more traumatic. This tradeoff meant that for some patients, the AneuRx procedure would be better, and for others, the best solution would be the silicon-fabric tube.[69]

The FDA article advocating for the synthetic fiber tube was peer-reviewed and used the same data, provided by the device's manufacturer, Medtronic. Not surprisingly, Medtronic vocally protested the article before it could be published. Medtronic put pressure on congressmen and the FDA to revoke the article as unfounded, although much of the evidence critical of the device company came from its own data.[70]

In 2003, before the article could be published, FDA leaders decided to pull it. Dan Shultz, the acting director of the FDA's Center for Devices and Radiological Health, "was told to write a letter to the medical journal requesting that the paper be withdrawn," according to Dr. Lazar Greenfield, professor of vascular surgery at the University of Michigan.[71] FDA leadership advised its own regulatory experts against publishing medical information that would have allowed doctors to provide better care for patients suffering from often fatal aortic aneurysms.

During this case of evidence suppression, FDA leadership maintained direct ties to the pharmaceutical industry. Before serving as the chief counsel to the FDA, Daniel Troy had made a career defending the Brown & Williamson Tobacco Corp and Pfizer Pharmaceuticals against federal regulators. When he changed careers and joined the FDA, *US News & World Report* ran the headline, "Mr. Outside Moves Inside: Daniel Troy Fought the FDA for Years; Now He's Helping to Run It."

During his first year as the FDA's chief counsel, Troy met with drug company representatives in over 50 closed-door meetings. When *US News* used the Freedom of Information Act to request records of the fifty-plus meetings between Troy and top pharmaceutical and device company officials, Troy's office responded that there were "no minutes, no memos, no nothing."

As chief counsel, Troy specifically asked the journal to pull the AneuRx article. Its authors felt that their professional duty had been compromised and publicly insisted that the FDA remain objective. The medical community offered sharp criticism, with one surgeon asking, "since when has the FDA begun telling medical journals what they can and can't publish?" On November 16, 2004, Troy resigned without explanation.[72]

Publication bias makes the average drug appear safer than it really is and encourages medical journals to bias positive results. Pharmaceutical industry influence on the FDA affects the majority of FDA drug approval decisions. By law, members of the FDA advisory committees, which play a major role in drug approval and review, are barred from receiving financial contributions from the companies of drugs under review. However, in practice, the FDA has the power to waive conflicts of interest in situations it deems appropriate. Between 1998 and the mid-2000s, the FDA waived more than 800 conflicts, creating bias in about 54 percent of regulator committees.[73] Waivers enable the FDA to feign the appearance of taking stringent measures against conflicts of interest, while still maintaining ties to the pharmaceutical industry.

In 2006, the FDA instituted a new rule that barred consultants on drug review panels from receiving more than $50,000 from pharmaceutical companies and prevented them from serving on drug approval panels. However, the $50,000 cap did not prohibit consultants from receiving $50,000 each from several different companies.[74]

Industry influence has repeatedly crept into the highest level of the FDA. Former FDA chief Lester M. Crawford pled guilty, in 2006, to concealing ownership in three health-related companies. Andrew von Eshenbach, who headed the FDA under George W. Bush, took a job with Greenleaf Health LLC in

2009.[75] Greenleaf is a consulting firm that advises pharmaceutical and device manufacturers on how to interact with regulators like the FDA.[76] Eschenbach's exact benefits are unknown, but he certainly received a significant increase in pay. In the balance between federal regulation and industry advocacy, it is important to keep in mind that the position of FDA chief pays around $150,000, while industry lobbyists often start at around $300,000.[77] [78]

Industry money also finds its way into the pockets of our elected representatives. In 2009, the New York Times revealed that four congressmen from New Jersey put "extreme" and "unusual" pressure on the FDA to approve a device called Menaflex. Menaflex is a C-shaped pad that is inserted into the knee to repair a damaged meniscus: the cushion between knee bones. A clinical trial suggested that the device is no more effective than routine surgery. Moreover, the device frequently fails, requiring follow-up surgeries.[79]

ReGen Biologics, the New Jersey company that manufactures Menaflex, paid $26,000 in campaign contributions to Senators Robert Menendez and Frank R. Lautenberg, and Representatives Frank Pallone, Jr., and Steven R. Rothman.[80] After receiving those contributions, these elected officials from New Jersey urged the FDA approve the device for the market. Their petition succeeded. FDA commissioner Dr. Andrew von Eschenbach supported the device's approval, even though Menaflex had for years been unanimously deemed ineffective by the agency's scientists. When the story broke, implicating ReGen, the New Jersey elected officials, and von Eschenbach were forced to resign. But not before the $3,000 device had been installed in the knees of thirty American patients and 3,000 Europeans.[81]

Researchers with direct ties to the pharmaceutical industry routinely advise the FDA to approve unsafe drugs. Consider the story of Rezulin, a diabetes drug manufactured by Warner-Lambert that first reached markets in 1997. Doctors would prescribe Rezulin to lower blood sugar levels in patients with adult-onset diabetes. However, the drug had significant side-effects, including liver damage and damage to the heart.

When FDA medical officer Dr. John Gueriguian reviewed Warner-Lambert's Rezulin approval application, he grew concerned about the harmful side effects and recommended that the application be denied. Warner-Lambert complained to Dr. Gueriguian's superiors and, in response, they removed Gueriguian from the project, eliminated his report from files, and denied the FDA advisory committees access to his negative findings.

Without a strong voice of impartial opposition, the FDA promptly approved Rezulin's application.[82] Soon after the drug reached markets, cases of liver failure began mounting on a massive scale. But just as concerns began to surface, the drug company dispatched its defenders. At first, an article published in the *New England Journal of Medicine* downplayed the dangers of Rezulin-induced liver failure, even though the side effects were well known. Later, a few researchers with funding ties to Warner-Lambert strongly advised the FDA against withdrawing the drug.

Following those recommendations, Rezulin stayed on the market for another 30 months. As complications from the drug continued, the Los Angeles Times tried to contact the deputy director of the FDA's Center for Drug Evaluation and Research, Dr. Murray Lumpkin. Lumpkin had advocated for keeping Rezulin on the market. However, he was unable to comment because he was on the French Riviera at a trade group conference put on by the pharmaceutical industry. Soon afterward, the FDA decided to pull Rezulin from the market. The dangerous drug had remained on the market two and a half years. By then, 90 people had suffered liver failure and 63 had died. Warner-Lambert made more than $1.8 billion in the process.[83]

Unfortunately, to this day, the FDA routinely approves unsafe drugs. As recently as 2012, the FDA approved a number of unsafe drugs from Bayer pharmaceuticals that increased the likelihood of fatal blood clots, deep vein thrombosis, and other serious medical problems. The drugs shared the common ingredient drospirenone, a synthetic hormone found in Bayer's birth control pills, Yaz and Yasmin and used by over four million women worldwide. They are Bayer's top-selling pharmaceutical products.[84]

Thousands of women filed a lawsuit against Bayer, citing injuries resulting from the two drugs. Amid growing controversy, the FDA convened a 26 member panel to investigate the evidence. Following its review, the panel voted 15-11 in favor of keeping the drugs on the market, but adding a warning label notifying consumers of increased likelihood of blood clots. The new labels may prevent lawsuits, but they do nothing to improve the safety of the drug.

Following the decision, the *Washington Monthly* and the *British Medical Journal* (*BMJ*) investigated the panel. They discovered that five of the committee members who had voted "yes" had direct financial ties to Bayer. Had those "yes" votes gone the other way, Yaz and Yasmin would not have stayed on the market.

Additionally, important documents were barred from the FDA panel's decision-making process. A report by David Kessler, former FDA commissioner and an expert witness in the lawsuits filed against Bayer, estimated that Yasmin causes a "several-fold increase" in blood clots compared to other oral contraceptives. It also concluded that Yasmin's rate of serious adverse effects was "10 fold higher" than that of other products. Furthermore, the report contained information suggesting that Bayer had failed to report these health concerns to the FDA. The company illegally promoted the drugs for off-label use, paying 450,000 to a gynecologist and author to promote the drugs during her book tour. However, the FDA prohibited Kessler's report from factoring into the review committee on the grounds that the date to submit documents had passed.

But while the FDA sanctioned bias in favor of the drug company, they censored its opposing voices.[85] Prominent consumer advocate, Sidney Wolfe was barred from serving on the FDA panel for his previous statements, critical of the drugs in question. Ironically, the FDA decided that he had an "intellectual conflict of interest."[86]

However, often the whistleblowers themselves are no more than the tools of outside interests. In the controversy surrounding Provenge, a drug and procedure involving the extraction and reintroduction of white blood cells as immunotherapy for prostate cancer, the FDA's chief independent analyst, Marie Huber acted as the representative of an asset management firm.[87] Though Huber declared no conflict of interest in the investigation, her resume, published by the whistle-blowing website: theprovengetrials.org, revealed that between January 2007 and January 2011 she worked for P. Schoenfeld Asset Management in New York. There, she held a position as a senior biotech analyst, where she made recommendations on the firm's trading strategies. According to an investment message board, the firm planned on short selling its share in the manufacturer of Provenge: the Dendreon Corp. Following Dr. Huber's ostensibly impartial recommendations, the FDA approved another competing prostate cancer drug, abiraterone acetate, brand name Zytiga. Meanwhile, in light of Huber's criticism, the stock price for Dendreon Corp plunged.[88] Quite often our "whistle blowers" blow the whistle to the tune of their own financial interests.

When it comes to our health, high level corporate manipulation exacts a terrible human cost. Industry money distorts what people accept as normal, and causes profound problems for the most vulnerable among us. Consider Attention Deficit Hyperactive Disorder (ADHD). The diagnosis indicates inattention, hyperactivity, and impulsiveness, and is often associated with the diagnosis of bipolar disorder, which is characterized by disruptive mood swings. Top ADHD psychiatric researchers at Harvard Medical School, Timothy E. Wilens and Dr. Joseph Biederman have for years encouraged doctors to diagnose bipolar disorder in children and prescribe antipsychotic drugs.[89] By 2004, doctors diagnosed about 40 times as many child ADHD cases as they did ten years prior, largely due to Biederman's efforts.[90]

Unfortunately, for some children, the antipsychotic stimulants have caused serious side effects. Two percent of children have undiscovered or unknown heart defects that make taking ADHD drugs deadly.[91] The FDA released a study showing that 19 children and 6 adults are known to have died from taking ADHD drugs during one four-year period, and 26 children either suffered strokes or abnormally fast heart rates.[92] The 50,000-80,000 children still taking the drugs remain at risk of sudden death.

Critics pressured the FDA to require a black warning label on the ADHD drug packaging so that parents would be aware of the dangers, but the FDA refused. In 2008, the American Heart Association recommended that all doctors administer electrocardiograms (EKGs) to children before prescribing ADHD stimulants or renewing prescriptions to prevent heart failure.[93] Wilens ridiculed the recommendation at an event funded by Abbot Laboratories, the pharmaceutical company that manufactures ADHD drugs.[94] Both Wilens and Biederman claimed they received "only" a few hundred thousand dollars each from the pharmaceutical companies that sold ADHD and antipsychotic drugs. In actuality, they were awarded a minimum of $1.6 million each.[95]

Often pharmaceutical companies pay licensed doctors to advocate for the use of FDA approved drugs for non-approved conditions, known as "off label" use. For instance, using a drug approved for diabetes to treat cancer. Pharmaceutical companies are prohibited by law from marketing their drugs directly for "off label" use and must rely on medical professionals to evangelize their campaign. The case of Biederman and Willens is just one instance in which physicians received payments to market dangerous psychoactive drugs for questionable cases of ADHD. This instance is only the tip of the iceberg.

In the case of the ADHD drug Ritalin, even schools should be held accountable for dangerous prescriptions promoted by the pharmaceutical industry. Matthew Smith was only 14 when he died suddenly after taking the drug for seven years. His parents had taken him to a doctor's office to get Ritalin on the advice of a counselor at Matthew's school. While hesitant, the school warned them that unless they medicated their son, Child Protective Services would prosecute both parents for neglect.

Matthew's school received extra funding for each child diagnosed with ADHD, which means that the school is financially incentivized to diagnose the disorder. However, many of the "symptoms" used in the diagnosis of ADHD are identical to the criteria for identifying gifted and talented children, including, for example, flights of ideas, hyperactivity, and distractibility.[96] With so much overlap, it is wrong to diagnose as many children with ADHD as we do, when in fact many of those children may be simply restless in classes below their ability.

Matthew was playing with his two cousins in his aunt's basement, when he suddenly fell off his skateboard. Paramedics took him to Royal Oak William Beaumont Hospital, where he was pronounced dead. Medical examiner Ljubisa Dragovic said that Smith had not died from the fall, but rather, "there was a chronic change of the heart muscle and the small blood vessels in the heart. This comes from long term exposure. This kid was on [Ritalin] repeatedly for 10 years."[97] A normal heart of an adult man weighs about 350 grams. Smith's 14-year-old heart weighed 402 grams.

With the proper screening, Matthew's life could have been saved. An electrocardiogram, or EKG, could have discovered the damage to his heart in time to switch medication and save his life from a medication that he may not have needed in the first place. In fact, the American Heart Association recommends that children receive an EKG before taking Ritalin.

However, some child psychiatrists oppose EKG screening. Dr. Steven Pliszka, a child psychiatrist at the University of Texas at San Antonio, joined Wilens and others in opposing EKGs. Pliszka claimed he was "baffled" by the American Heart Association recommendation, and said he would refuse to use EKG as a screening tool.[98] Pliszka argues that children taking Ritalin are not at more risk for heart problems than those not taking the drugs, despite evidence to the contrary. Pliszka also argues that an EKG screening process could deter parents from seeking treatment for their children, because getting an EKG means added expense and hassle.[99]

Unsurprisingly, Pliszka received money from companies that manufacture ADHD medication. ADHD manufacturers fund his research and, in addition, Pliszka has served as a consultant for ADHD drug manufacturers.[100] The for-profit medical system has created untrustworthy experts. The problem is all too common for patients with mental illness, especially among children who have no say in the decision.

In no other sector of our economy do such egregious instances of professional bias persist, especially when they endanger human life. However, by pointing fingers at individual physicians, we are wasting time. Some individuals are to blame, surely, but the problem is systemic. So long as the profit motive guides the decisions of health care corporations to influence our providers, we should expect the catastrophe to continue.

Buckling Under the Muscle of the Pharmaceutical Industry

Beyond individual cases, the power of pharmaceutical influence has muscled its way into our nation's largest health care legislation. To ensure the passage of the Affordable Care Act (ACA), the Obama administration made a secret deal with the pharmaceutical industry. The administration agreed that Medicaid would not negotiate cheaper drug prices or reimport less expensive drugs from Canada. In return, the pharmaceutical industry agreed to commit $80 billion in support of the bill.[101] Here is the leaked memo detailing the agreement: [102]

July 7 --

PhRMA DEAL
Commitment of up to $80 billion, but not more than $80 billion.
1. Agree to increase of Medicaid rebate from 15.1 - 23.1% ($34 billion)
2. Agree to get FOBs done (but no agreement on details -- express disagreement on data exclusivity which both sides say does not affect the score of the legislation.) ($9 billion)
3. Sell drugs to patients in the donut hole at 50% discount ($25 billion)
This totals $68 billion
4. Companies will be assessed a tax or fee that will score at $12 billion. There was no agreement as to how or on what this tax/fee will be based.
Total: $80 billion

In exchange for these items, the White House agreed to:
1. Oppose importation
2. Oppose rebates in Medicare Part D
3. Oppose repeal of non-interference
4. Oppose opening Medicare Part B

On June 3, 2009, an unnamed pharmaceutical industry lobbyist e-mailed Nancy-Ann DeParle, Obama's former Deputy Chief of Staff for Policy. The lobbyist wanted reassurance that the White House would take no actions cutting into industry profits. DeParle responded that the administration had "made [its] decision, based on how constructive you guys have been, to oppose importation" on another issue.[103] Though perhaps a necessary compromise, this deal has essentially given the pharmaceutical industry free range to continue it harmful practices at a high cost to the patient.

With this agreement in place, the pharmaceutical industry came to support the ACA because it expanded the industry's customer base without lowering prices.[104] Richard Kirsch, a senior fellow at the Roosevelt Institute, argued that if the pharmaceutical industry had fought the ACA instead of supporting it, the bill would have probably never passed.[105]

Information and Misinformation

[A] patient faced with his own mortality has had the ground cut out from under him. Shocked, in pain, and facing enormous uncertainty, he may well want to put his life in the hands of an experienced and knowledgeable professional.

– Maggie Mahar, *Money Driven Medicine.*[106]

IN NO OTHER INDUSTRY IS THE DIVIDE IN KNOWLEDGE SO wide, and the information so critical, as in health care. Imagine that a doctor recommends a patient for coronary bypass surgery. How can the patient know if surgery is truly necessary, or if it will end up being one of the estimated 7.5 million unnecessary surgeries performed in the United States each year?[107] Some doctors pushing unnecessary coronary bypass surgeries have told patients they will die if they do not undergo surgery immediately.[108] Patients in this situation may be frightened and overwhelmed. Many simply cannot be expected to make rational decisions. Additionally, patients lack the knowledge of physiology and medicine to make informed choices that might deviate from their doctors' advice. And even if they ask for a second opinion, patients will most likely run up against another doctor who will recommend the same surgery, not wanting to contradict a colleague.

The sheer depth in the knowledge divide between medical professionals and their patients, distorts the proper function of the market for medical care. The efficiency of the free market system comes from the power of our collective decision making. In order for the decisions of many consumers to regulate the market effectively, they must be adequately informed on the implications of their choices. Without accessible and unbiased information, consumer decisions fail to optimize the quality of goods and services. In health care, the power of decentralized consumer input has been rendered useless.

George Akerlof, winner of the 2001 Nobel Prize in Economics, outlined the problem of market failure brought on by information asymmetry in his famous 1970 paper, "The Market for 'Lemons': Quality Uncertainty and the Market Mechanism." He invited the reader to imagine a simplified market for used cars. He described an uncertain "market in which...quality may be represented, or it may be misrepresented. The presence of people...who are willing to offer inferior goods tends to drive the market out of existence," as "dishonest dealings tend to drive honest dealings out of the market."[109]

In Akerlof's model, buyers assume they are getting a bad deal. As a result, the average price of used cars drops, and so does the average quality, as sellers of good quality cars leave the market.

In the case of the American market for health care, we find the opposite problem. Given its necessity and technical complexity, people assume that medicine is of a higher quality, even when they receive 'lemons.' Hence we end up paying a high cost for below average services. The health care market has been flooded with 'lemons,' but people still assume that American health care is the best in the world. As advancements in medical technology progress, the knowledge divide will only widen further, driving up costs into the future.

The dramatic asymmetry of information between patients and doctors permits practices of widespread abuse. Two doctors based in Redding, California recently performed more than 500 unnecessary heart surgeries in four years, telling their patient that they would die if they did not immediately consent to surgery.

Steven Hunt described his experience at Redding hospital in an interview with Maggie Mahar, the author of *Money Driven Medicine*: "if I waited, the doctor told me, I could have a heart attack just walking across the hospital parking lot. And, because of where the problem was in my heart, I could die. They gave me no choice but to do the operation. Do it or die."

At least three physicians warned the hospital that something was wrong, but the hospital, which was making millions of dollars on the surgeries, refused to investigate. Meanwhile, the doctors had so many scheduled surgeries that they had to rush in some procedures. Ultimately, the scheme jeopardized patients and wasted hospital resources, not to mention the more than 500 lawsuits and criminal investigation that followed. Ironically, for five years in a row, the hospital's cardiac treatment center received a five star rating from HealthGrades, a health care information company.[110]

Shirley Wooten, 79, visited her doctor at the Redding Medical Center for a slight pain in her left shoulder. After performing an initial examination, her doctor insisted she undergo double bypass surgery the next day. Reluctant, but frightened, she agreed to the procedure. During the operation, her doctor made a mistake and she almost bled to death. After all-night surgery to repair the damage done by the first operation, she was expected to die. She surprised her doctors by surviving, but spent a month in the ICU and has never regained her sense of balance.[111] It turns out the surgery was never necessary in the first place and those operating on her made recommendations based on incentives to maximize their incomes. They were inclined to zealously interpret trivial preliminary signs as warranting surgery. While it may have helped the hospital make money in the short term, this instance of fraud almost cost Wooten her life. She represented a profit opportunity, and neither she nor her husband knew enough about medicine to protect her from her own doctors.

Pharmaceutical Deception

Lack of information also allows the pharmaceutical industry to push for the development and sale of virtually useless and redundant drugs. In 1992, when the FDA last classified the therapeutic gain of approved drugs, more than half offered "little or no therapeutic gain." Up until 1992, the FDA categorized drugs into three groups: those giving important therapeutic gains, those giving modest therapeutic gains, and those giving little or no therapeutic gains. Drugs in this third category tend to be slight modifications on existing drugs.

FDA Category	Number	Percent
Important Therapeutic Gains	41	16 percent
Modest Therapeutic Gain	80	31 percent
Little or No Therapeutic Gain	137	53 percent

FDA drug categorization, 1982-1991. Ranking system abolished in 1992.

In response to the ranking system, the pharmaceutical industry launched an intense lobbying campaign and in 1992, they succeeded in abolishing it. In a shocking display of hubris, John Stafford, CEO of American Home Products, said that "to put the [classification system] into well-deserved oblivion was a priority [of the Pharmaceutical Manufacturers Association] for a very long time." Their persistence and success has allowed pharmaceutical companies to spend resources on negligible improvements in current medicine.

Spokespeople for the pharmaceutical industry systematically exaggerate the cost of bringing new drugs to market, in order to justify high drug prices. The most recent pharmaceutical industry estimate in 2006, put the cost of bringing one new drug to market at $1.32 billion. Adjusted for inflation in today's terms, that estimated cost is now approaching $2 billion.[112] Alan Holmer, president of the Pharmaceutical Research and Manufacturers of America (PhRMA), claimed that if we were to lower drug prices, we would "harm millions of Americans who have life-threatening conditions."[113]

However, independent sources have put the pharmaceutical industry's figures to the test and found that the real median cost of bringing a drug to market is only about $55 million.[114]

Pharmaceutical industry spokespeople justify the high price of their products by grossly exaggerating their R& D costs by an exponential amount. It is no wonder that our own pharmaceutical industry is able to sell the same drugs in Canada and Europe for less than half the price charged in the United States.

An investigation of the industry's budget unearthed various strategies employed by the industry to artificially inflate its R&D costs. Pharmaceutical companies have systematically mislabeled marketing costs as R&D, as R&D may be written off as a tax break. They have kept their methods of evaluating costs a secret with the goal of distorting their expenditures in favor of R&D over marketing.[115]

Behind the industry spin, the real budget tells a different story. In an article published by the Boston Medical Journal, Donal Light and J.R. Lexchin point out that for every dollar pharmaceutical companies spend on R&D, they spend $19 on promotion and marketing.[116] Globally, the pharmaceutical industry spends one-third of its revenue on marketing, including direct to patient TV marketing, which comes to over $290 billion dollars every year. The illusion of high R&D costs also allows the pharmaceutical industry to conceal its tremendous CEO salaries and perks.[117]

CEO	Company	Salary 2011
William Weldon	Johnson & Johnson	$26,700,000
Ian Read	Pfizer	$25,000,000
Miles White	Abbott Laboratories	$24,000,000
Robert Coury	Mylan	$21,300,000
Kevin Sharer	Amgen	$18,900,000
John Lechleiter	Eli Lilly	$16,400,000
Joseph Jimenez	Novartis	$15,700,000
John Martin	Gilead	$15,600,000
Lamberto Andreotti	Bristol-Myers Squibb	$14,900,000
Robert Parkinson	Baxter	$14,100,000

Top ten pharmaceutical company CEO salaries, 2011.[118]

In her book, *The Truth About the Drug Companies*, Marcia Angell reveals that upon his 2001 retirement, the Chairman of Bristol-Myers Squibb, Charles Heimbold, Jr, received a salary of $74,890,918, plus $76,095,611 in unexercised stock options.[119] Mylan CEO Robert Coury spent $535,590 in company funds on personal vacations that included the use of Mylan's private jet.[120] Though the companies reported expenditures might suggest otherwise, it is safe to assume that Mr. Coury was not conducting R&D.

The pharmaceutical industry pays lobbyists to keep industry R&D costs secret, even from the US government. In 1972, the US General Accounting Office (GAO) initiated a comprehensive study of the pharmaceutical industry, in order to gauge its profitability and amount of competition. In particular, the GAO wanted access to industry data that would allow it to estimate industry spending on R&D, marketing, promotion, and distribution. When the GAO approached the industry with its request, it was met with tremendous resistance.

Lawyers spent the next nine years on a series of legal battles over one statute's wording. The debate centered on whether distinguishing between R&D and marketing cost was "directly" or "indirectly" pertinent to the GAO's investigation.[121] Between 1977 and 1983, the outcome of ten separate Federal court cases favored the pharmaceutical industry. Finally, in April 1983, the Supreme Court ruled in favor of the pharmaceutical companies by a seven to two vote. Ultimately, the decision barred the GAO from accessing data on the industry's R&D costs, deeming those figures were not directly pertinent to the investigation. Now, a congressional subpoena is the only way to access budgetary data on the pharmaceutical industry.[122] Recently, the national nonprofit consumer advocacy organization Public Citizen subpoenaed the industry data. Their efforts revealed that the actual cost of bringing a new drug to market is only around $55 million; a figure just 24 times short of $1.32 billion, the last figure claimed by the industry.[123]

Through manipulation, the pharmaceutical industry has managed to maintain extraordinarily high profit margins. As of 2012, pharmaceutical industry profit margins stood at around 30 percent.[124] By comparison, commercial banking ranked second at 13.5 percent, and the median return across all other industries stood at just 3.3 percent of sales. Annual industry revenue now tops out at $330 billion in the United States, and over $880 billion globally.[125]

With no mechanisms to ensure transparency, disguising marketing costs as R&D is a perfectly reasonable corporate strategy for a maximizing profit. Nevertheless, the public has no idea whether the high prices for drugs, devices, and tests are justified.

Fraud and Abuse

THE FRAGMENTED NATURE OF THE US HEALTH CARE SYSTEM exempts any one party from full responsibility. Though a doctor may be directly responsible for a botched surgery, it is the fragmented nature of the system that allows the interests of pharmaceuticals and insurance companies to escape responsibility.

We need legislation that makes government and corporate activity transparent, and makes that information public. At present, one may only access some of this information through filing a request with the Freedom of Information Act, a cumbersome and rarely employed process.

Unpunished Fraud

Unpunished fraud is another way in which our for-profit health care system fails to account for our high cost of care.

In her book *Money-Driven Medicine: The Real Reason Health Care Costs So Much*, Maggie Mahar tells the story of a doctor at a hospital in Pennsylvania who discovered that in between surgeries, many anesthesiologists left their patients in the care of a nurse anesthetist. Effectively, the doctors were subcontracting their responsibilities to the nurses. Though cost effective for the hospital and the doctors, this practice carried dangers for the patients, who weren't getting the level treatment that their situations demanded. One physician, Dr. Ed Dench, protested, refusing to participate in the practice. He warned his colleagues against billing for operations in which they weren't completely present. Though the physicians were clearly committing Medicare fraud, the practice refused to investigate. Not only that, the hospital launched an investigation on Dr. Dench, in search of a reason to dismiss him. Eventually, the inevitable tragedy happened; some patients died because the physician anesthesiologists were not present during the surgery. The hospital was sued. Instead of rewarding Dr. Dench for advocating patient safety, the hospital fired him from the anesthesiology department.[126]

Even for experts, estimating the total cost of health care fraud in America has proved difficult, and produced varied, sometimes conflicting results. A few key factors make it hard to estimate the total cost of fraud. For one, the private sector is under no legal obligation to report fraud figures. Furthermore, fraudulent practices are difficult to detect because many of them are deceptively simple. They include small acts of work related negligence, as in the case of anesthesiologists who left nurses to do their work in between surgeries. Insurance companies pay physicians for their expertise, even when their expertise is not actually involved.

Finally, fraud can be defined in many different ways, producing varied estimates. Some define fraud as "knowingly and willfully executing, or attempting to execute, a scheme or ploy to defraud the Medicare program." Others include abuse in their fraud estimates, defining abuse as practices that are inconsistent with standard procedures for providing care. Still others include waste in their fraud estimates, including inefficiency, unnecessary or prolonged treatments, and any money spent on health care that could be eliminated without reducing the quality of care.[127]

Authoritative estimates put national, annual health care fraud costs in the hundreds of billions, and even trillions of dollars. In 2008, the Health Research Institute, a branch of the accounting firm PricewaterhouseCoopers, published a report that estimated total annual fraud costs, including waste, at $1.2 trillion. That year, the total health care spending in the United States was $2.2 trillion, meaning that more than half of all health care spending was fraud and waste.[128] Of course, here we are not including the human cost of pain, suffering, and even death.

In 2009, Thomas Reuters reported its own estimate of health care fraud. The estimate included fraud, abuse, and "waste," which the study defined as health care costs that can be eliminated without reducing quality. The study produced a figure between $600 and $850 billion each year. Subtracting waste, Thomson Reuters reported between $125 and $175 billion in fraud and abuse.[129]

The FBI assumes that fraudulent billing accounts for between 3 and 10 percent of total health care expenditures, both public and private. On that assumption, we can estimate that fraud and abuse account for between $75 and $250 billion each year. The FBI does not include waste in its estimates.[130] Its definition only refers to legally provable cases. Most fraud and abuse, like the case of the dermatologist that treated a single wart for eight months and charged $1,200, cannot be proven, and will go undetected.

Although the exact value for the total amount of money wasted by American health care is by nature elusive, it is certainly in the high hundreds of billions, if not trillions of dollars. If we cut all waste and fraud we would be able to insure our entire population two times over, with each person paying half the current price. We, the taxpayers, pay for much of those wasted billions. Consider that the sum of the budgets for Medicare and Medicaid is roughly $900 billion. It is a shame that in the present system, nearly half of the budget pays for waste.[131]

Fraud legal settlements are on the rise. The Department of Justice reports that a typical fraud case now involves a settlement between $30 and $50 million. In her extensive analysis on Medicare Fraud, Nancy Aldrich notes that ten years ago, a fraud case involving $1 million would have been seen as significant. Today it would hardly make the news.[132]

The following table contains the ten largest settlements reached between pharmaceutical companies and the United States Department of Justice between the years 1991 and 2012, ranked beginning with the highest settlement.

Company	Settlement	Violation(s)	Year	Product(s)
GlaxoSmith-Kline	$3 billion	Off-label promotion/failure to disclose safety data	2012	Avandia, Wellbutrin, Paxil
Pfizer	$2.3 billion	Off-label promotion/kickbacks	2009	Bextra, Geodon, Zyvox, Lyrica
Abbot Laboratories	$1.5 billion	Off-label promotion	2012	Depakote
Eli Lilly	$1.4 billion	Off-label promotion	2009	Zyprexa
TAP Pharmaceutical Products	$875 million	Medicare fraud/ kickbacks	2001	Lupron
Amgen	$762 million	Off-label promotion/kickbacks	2012	Aranesp
GlaxoSmith-Kline	$750 million	Poor manufacturing practices	2010	Kytril, Bactroban, Paxil CR, Avandamet
Serono	$704 million	Off-label promotion/kickbacks/ monopoly practices	2005	Serostim
Merck	$650 million	Medicare fraud/ kickbacks	2008	Zocor, Vioxx, Pepsid
Purdue Pharma	$601 million	Off-label promotion	2007	Oxycontin

Ten largest fraud settlements between pharmaceutical companies and the United States Department of Justice, 1991-2012, ranked by settlement amount, highest to lowest. GlaxoSmithKline (2012),[133] Pfizer,[134] Abbot Laboratories,[135] Eli Lilly,[136] TAP Pharmaceutical Products,[137] Amgen,[138] GlaxoSmithKline (2010),[139] Serono,[140] Merck,[141] Purdue Pharma.[142]

Behind these settlement numbers, we find hundreds of thousands of patients who have suffered debilitating injury and loss of life, not measurable in dollars. Using the False Claims Act, individual whistleblowers working with the Department of Justice, recover only a small portion of the nation's total medical fraud each year. These recoveries tend to total in the low single digit billions. In 2010, the Department of Justice recovered $2.5 billion in fraud, the largest health care settlement in its history.[143] We cannot expect pharmaceutical companies to stop committing fraud on their own. Rather, they will do what has proved profitable. They will budget for it.

Of course, we should not single out pharmaceutical companies alone, as hospitals, doctors, equipment manufacturers, testing facilities, surgery centers, rehab centers, dialysis units, and many others contribute a considerable share of fraud, abuse, and waste.

One recent case of widespread fraud orchestrated by DaVita, a kidney dialysis company, highlights the systemic nature of intentional deception. In 2012, an investigative report conducted by "The Situation Room with Wolf Blitzer," exposed the widespread and intentional underuse of resources at the company's 2,000 kidney dialysis clinics. Two plaintiffs alleged that providers dispensed only a small portion of the medication contained in glass vials and discarded the rest, while still charging patients for the entire bottle. Similar companies ordered smaller bottles of the medication, but used the entirety of its contents. Over the course of several years, DaVita charged Medicare and Medicaid $800 million for mostly unused drugs.[144]

In May 2009, a California doctor was sentenced to 16 years in prison for intentionally performing unnecessary surgeries in a fraud scheme worth $154 million. The three doctors implicated in the conspiracy performed a total of 1,037 unnecessary procedures. They performed unnecessary surgeries for sweaty hands and failed to follow basic patient safety protocol. "A sweaty palm surgery requires a patient to undergo general anesthesia, where the doctor will collapse a lung to clamp a nerve right next to the spine," said District Attorney Tony Rackauckas. "It is dangerous, almost always unnecessary, and may result in terrible side effects. It is outrageous that a doctor would cut into healthy patients and use their bodies as cash registers."[145]

Some patients were in on the scheme and received payments in exchange for undergoing surgery. Insurance fraud middlemen called "cappers" brought the patients to the surgeons for $2,000 apiece, altogether earning about $1 million.[146] One of the cappers, Sue Nanda, recruited over 170 patients from 16 states, none of whom needed surgery. Nanda arranged the transportation of patients, the scheduling of surgeries, and coached the healthy patients on what to say. She had them sign false affidavits stating that they had not received any form of compensation for the surgeries they would receive. However, the patients received between $300 and $1,000 per surgery, or credit towards cosmetic surgery.[147]

"Upcoding" is another common fraudulent practice in our for-profit system that allows physicians to mark up costs, without providing additional services. Normally, procedures and medications are billed according to codes set by insurance companies and government agencies. Because the codes permit some leeway in charging decisions, there is a real incentive for medical professionals to "upcode" procedures and products, by selecting codes corresponding to higher values for equivalent services. An entire class of coding specialists makes money by "upcoding" bills and overcharging Medicare, Medicaid, and insurance companies. Upcoding takes two forms: either diagnosing at a higher code level, or choosing more expensive treatments. The highest-billing code may not correspond with the best treatment, but the provider is incentivized to select it anyway.

Understanding the vast array of problems that arise in our for-profit health care system can be overwhelming. Currently, no profit motivated health delivery system adequately prioritizes the patient. Our health is dictated by profit maximizing corporate interests with the power to influence our doctors and withhold vital information. Even medical education has been corrupted by misinformation, used to promote the most heavily funded and lucrative products. Access to accurate information is the basic requirement of any market pretending to be responsive to the forces of consumer demand. By not addressing the corruption of consumer knowledge, we allow the persistence of massive market failures in our nation's most vital industry. Moreover, our system of malpractice only serves to hold doctors accountable for individual cases, effectively pardoning the true culprits. Our doctors continue to take the fall for decisions made in corporate board rooms.

Statistics do not lie. The high cost of health care does not reflect our quality of health. We pay twice as much as most other developed countries and receive the lowest quality care. Unnecessary surgeries and tests, permeated with billions in fraudulent billing, drives up prices and put our wellbeing in danger. Pharmaceutical companies overcharge us for often harmful drugs and use the profits to develop and market minor improvements on existing products. Piecemeal legislation will never be enough to fix the depth of the problem. We need systemic change to consolidate the scattered parts of our health care system into a health maximizing nonprofit cooperative.

THE SOLUTION

Cooperative Health Care

ONLY BY REMOVING THE PROFIT MOTIVE WILL WE SUCCEED in alleviating the symptoms of our dysfunctional health care system. Not only is access to health a right, but placing a premium on profit has severely crippled efficiency and innovation in this sector of our economy. When a market ceases to prioritize the value it provides to its customers, it must be fundamentally restructured. We need a solution that incentivizes our doctors to put patient care before any monetary motivation.

Thanks to the circumstances of our time, we are well poised to make lasting improvements in our health care delivery system. In the last two years, all three branches of our government have debated and endorsed a massive step in the right direction. The Affordable Care Act (ACA) addresses a portion of the problem by establishing a nonprofit insurance agency. However, the program only serves to eliminate the profit motive from one sector of the industry. The ACA does not limit the influence that for-profit corporations hold over how our legislators, regulators, and doctors make decisions about our health.

We need a plan that puts the right pressure on physicians and surgeons to use the most effective methods at their disposal, rather than the most profitable ones. To do so, we must merge the various parts of the health care system, in order to channel their fragmented interests towards the single motivation of patient care. At present, we should take advantage of our forward momentum, by expanding the nonprofit insurance company within the ACA, into a nonprofit health care provider. We must put pressure on our elected officials to amend the ACA, to grant the nonprofit insurance company mandated in the present law the option to expand its charter.

A Vision for Nonprofit Health Care

WE PROPOSE A NATIONAL NONPROFIT COOPERATIVE TO ACT not just as an insurance company, but as a comprehensive health care provider. The organization will be designed to eliminate professional conflicts of interest, reduce the incentive for doctors and corporations to exploit the knowledge gap with patients, and ensure accountability across all sectors. Under the cooperative, doctors will be salaried and their pay increases will be based on performance. Pharmaceuticals will be purchased at bulk prices, conflicting financial ties to for-profit health care companies will be prohibited and strictly enforced, and management will be accountable to the direct vote of those purchasing insurance policies with the cooperative. All funding for the cooperative will come from insurance policies, which cover patient needs without bias against preexisting conditions.

The proposed nonprofit co-op will be therapeutic, with a focus on cost saving preventive measures, rather than expensive and often dangerous treatments and procedures. Not only will this cooperative solution improve our nation's health, it will save our economy a sum of money greater than twice the value of our entire defense budget.

The private co-op will function similar to a health care maintenance organization (HMO), such as Kaiser, but will be truly nonprofit. Any excess funds will be returned to policy purchasers or used to improve patient care. Doctor's raises will be based on positive feedback from peer and patient evaluations.

Management of the agency will be guided by a board of directors, elected by the vote of the policy holders. The co-op bylaws will treat its policy holders, as stakeholders, and as such grants them the right to elect members to the board.

The most fundamental function of the co-op will be to set the right incentives for its health providers. To do so, the organization will employ a carrot and stick approach based on the quality of care. In her book, *Who Killed Health Care?*, Harvard economist, Regina Herzlinger explains the logic of creating consumer-driven incentives in the market for health care. "Ideological advocates of consumer-driven health care invoke the mystical, invisible-hand powers of free markets. But effective markets do not work through ideology." She argues that in many cases, we must actively define the incentives in order to best address the needs of the consumer. Her research indicates that "in behavioral economics, when punishment and loss of reputation were combined, they resulted in the highest production of public goods."[148] Drawing from this research, the co-op will tie the reputation and pay of its doctors to consumer based evaluations.

Salary contracts for doctors will be determined based on a survey of the national average income of physician, surgeons, and other specialty providers. Bonuses will incentivize quality care, and penalties will discourage suboptimal care. Starting pay will be 25 percent higher than those set by the open market. If an average specialist makes $200,000 per year, the health care co-op will pay $250,000. Tremendous cost savings on drugs, insurance structure, administrative budgeting, overutilization, and fraud will enable the co-op to pay doctors a higher salary than any for-profit HMO. Through better salaries, the co-op will attract and retain the best talent. Contracts for all employees of the cooperative health provider will include clear prohibitions against holding financial stake in the for-profit health care industry. This prohibition will be broad, transparent, and vigorously enforced.

As the co-op will manage the entire process from selling insurance to paying doctors and contracting with hospitals, no additional funding will originate from the for-profit medical sector. Access to cheaper drugs and devices, chosen without conflicting financial interests, will enable doctors to make the best possible decisions.

Employers who choose to buy policies through the co-op, will pay less and provide better health benefits for their employees. Businesses purchasing plans from the co-op will save on their own budgets and those without health plans will be encouraged to do so by this affordable option.

The co-op presents the federal government with an opportunity to save enormous amounts of money on its most expensive entitlement programs. By contracting with the co-op for all policies covered under Medicare, Medicaid, and SCHIP, the government will save a conservative estimate of $420 billion annually. In 2012, these programs cost the government $827; the co-op will effectively cut the burden of those obligations in half. At the same time, this initial contract will supply the co-op with a large initial customer base. Its size, will enable the co-op to better negotiate bulk purchases with pharmaceutical and medical device companies.

The co-op will offer various policy options. A) Basic Coverage will include emergency services, other essential services, prescription drugs, devices, and preventive care. At present, Medicare and Medicaid cover the amenities listed in the co-op's Basic Coverage package. B) Premier Coverage will include additional non-essential services, such as cosmetic surgery, access to private hospital rooms, in addition to Basic Coverage. C) A third option will be a custom plan, somewhere between Basic Coverage and Premier Coverage. Any policyholder may elect to expand their coverage beyond the basic plan to include additional amenities and procedures, on an itemized basis. Every type of coverage will provide policyholders with the choice of adequate care or better, with a strong emphasis on preventive measures.

The co-op will eliminate copays, making doctor visits affordable and encouraging policy holders to undergo preliminary screenings to catch an ailment when it first arises. To discourage overuse, the co-op will charge a small fee, when the patient initiates the appointment themselves. No fee will be charged, for appointments initiated by doctors and other health care providers.

Everyone will have the option of buying a plan with the co-op, but no one will be required to choose it over an existing for-profit alternative, unless they currently receive care through Medicare, Medicaid, or SCHIP. The government will buy policies for individuals covered by those three programs and these individuals will also become voting members of the co-op. Individuals and businesses not covered by government programs will be able to buy policies at the same low cost paid by the government.

Excess revenue generated by premiums will be held in a contingency fund to finance bonuses for the co-op's providers and malpractice claims, and beyond that, will be returned to policy purchasers as a rebate, or used to improve the level of care. Premiums paid by individuals and employers will be tax deductible.

Basic Management Structure

The federal government will have no hand in managing the nonprofit co-op, with the exception of appointing one board member. This separation between the co-op and government will ensure that the co-op does not become burdened by bureaucratic inefficiency akin to "socialized medicine." It will remain a private, people-managed, nonprofit insurance co-op and health care provider.

Management of the co-op will have two tiers. At the top, a board of directors elected by policyholders will set strategy for the co-op's health provisions. The board will consist of seven elected professionals with extensive experience in managing large health care organizations. The directors will oversee and approve large contracts with government, major corporations, and employers. To administer the day-to-day operation of the co-op, the board will appoint several executive managers. A large staff of sub-managers will coordinate the billing process, contract for hospital and clinic space, and handle employee payroll.

The board of directors will oversee agency policies and management. The board will serve as a guide and watchdog for the decisions made by the managers. Board membership will be decided by a combination of three factors. Five members will be elected by the direct vote of the policyholders, one will be appointed by the government, and another will represent the employers who have purchased coverage packages for their employees. Candidates for election to the board must be nominated by existing board members or a minimum number of policyholders. Members of the board of directors will serve for four years, but every two years, half the members will be reelected, as in the US Senate. This overlapping arrangement will provide continuity, as well as a steady influx of new people and ideas. Board members will not be allowed to campaign for election and may only serve two terms for a total of eight years.

The board will also set management compensation. Executive managers will receive annual bonuses not exceeding their annual salary, upon recommendation of the board of directors and approval of the majority of co-op voting members. Salary caps on managers will serve as an additional check against overspending. The typical manager salary will be no higher than the highest paid government employee, the President.

The board of directors and its managers will be barred from holding financial stake in the for-profit health care industry. Strict prohibitions will prevent decision-makers and upper-management employees from taking jobs or otherwise receiving financial compensation from pharmaceutical companies, medical equipment companies, biotech companies, hospitals, nursing homes, lobbying groups, and other for-profit entities. The prohibition will hold for board members for a minimum of four years, and will extend to board members' family, trusts, and trustees. This prohibition will apply to all decision makers in the co-op's upper echelon responsible for executing agency policies, and awarding contracts.

Right, not Commodity

LET'S END A DEBATE. IN OUR LAST NATIONAL DISCUSSION ON health care, we argued extensively on whether access to health services should be treated as a right or a commodity. The outcome of the debate proved unclear. Consequently, the ACA, the system that arose from the debate defined health both as a right and as a commodity, in different instances. This incomplete approach fails to properly establish our right to health. Those favoring health as a commodity argue that the price of health care should be set by free market forces. They claim that declaring a national right to health is complicated by the need to provide access to the entitlement of health services. Since everyone's health needs are different, we cannot possibly universalize such a variable good. This logic is both flawed and contradictory. It disregards the founding precepts of our constitution, limits our freedom to choose the best care, and betrays the very definition of a commodity.

The United States recognized "life, liberty, and the pursuit of happiness," as the founding precepts of democratic society. The state exists to ensure these rights, if anything at all. As health is essential to life, not guaranteeing access to care for certain citizens, preferences death over our most fundamental right. Health and sanity are also indispensable to our most basic physical and mental liberty. As Jennifer Ruger, a professor at the Yale School of Public Health explains in her discussion on Aristotle's reasoning on freedom and health, "if a set of functions, such as the ability to feed oneself and walk unaided, constitute a person's well-being, then the capability to achieve those functions will constitute the person's freedom to have well-being."[149] In other words, with good health comes the freedom to perform and endure. Additionally, wellness of body and mind promotes our natural happiness stronger than any material possession. In good health, we are free to pursue the things we enjoy. If the US fails to guarantee adequate care for all its citizens, it has failed to honor its founding principles.

The connection between the 'right to life' and the 'right to health,' reflects a broad legal consensus. In a survey of all international cases involving the right to health, researchers at the WHO found that 83 percent of favorable rulings, cited the 'right to life' as the basis for the 'right to health,' regardless of whether health was outlined directly in the country's constitution.[150]

Those who oppose defining health as right, tend to argue that doing so is impossible because it requires an entitlement to health care services. As Dr. Eibe Reidel of the UN Commission on Economic, Social, and Cultural Rights explains, "the right to health also embraces an entitlement to a system of health care protection."[151] Hence, 'health as a right' has become entangled in the larger debate on the role of government. However, it is the duty of our government, as enshrined in our constitution, to ensure the right to human life. Our right to life inherently necessitates our right to health. Moreover, the 'right to health' and 'health care' are indispensable to each other. Justifying access to health care requires declaring a 'right to health,' while ensuring the 'right to health' requires policies that provide universal access to health care. The 'right to health' is intrinsic and the 'right to health care' is instrumental, meaning one guides and the other implements. In brief, guaranteeing our right to life requires a right to health care.

As the US has a strong tradition of favoring free market approaches, we often perceive guarantees of universal access to health care as contradicting the freedom of individuals to pursue health related decisions on their own terms.[152] In this sense, requiring a specific option would limit an individual's ability to select the best possible choice to fit his or her circumstances. While there may be some theoretical merit to this argument, in reality, the high cost of health care in our current system is extremely prohibitive. More than 40 million uninsured Americans are forced to forgo preventive treatments due to the high cost of for-profit private insurance. As a result, the freedom of many to choose the best care is limited to emergency services. The spirit of individualism espoused by our founding fathers has been unjustly confined to long waits in emergency rooms and thousand dollar procedures.

Furthermore, those able to afford regular care and a doctor of their choice have no way of definitively determining the effectiveness of prescribed treatments. Though the patient may use some indicator, such as price and reputation to determine their quality of care, their methods cannot account for the vast amount of professional deception. Public information available on the internet has made it easier for us to screen for the best quality of care, but at the point of service, the outcome of a procedure becomes uncertain. A misinformed choice is essentially the same as an uninformed choice. In this sense, our ability to make effective decisions based on quality has been severely diminished, and any semblance of beneficial free market forces has been rendered useless.

In stark contrast with the definition of a right, a commodity is a widely available economic good or service, exchangeable on an open market. Due to their near universal availability and need, commodities are priced solely by factors of supply and demand, rather than issues of quality. Limited differences in quality prevent producers from charging extra for their commodity, hence reducing the amount of profit that any one provider is able to make.

Commodities imply a sense of non-differentiation, meaning they are no different regardless of who provides them. Buying gasoline from Chevron is no different from purchasing it at Shell. The only real factor influencing our decisions is its price and location. The very opposite is true for health. Given the complexities of surgical operations and drug development, their quality can be extremely variable. Beyond price, the type of care is extremely important. Both the patient's ability to choose the best health care option and the doctors ability to perform it correctly, directly affects the patients quality of health. For this reason, many patients facing serious conditions often opt to receive surgery in faraway clinics that offer the specific type of care they desire. While our actual ability to determine the quality of our health care is limited by our own knowledge of medicine, we still act based on factors other than price alone. For this reason, our health is not a commodity.

Moreover, as anesthesiologist Dr. Robert Burney points out, "[i]n any other industry, when goods and services reach commodity status, the price comes down. This has not been true in health care, primarily because there is no price competition. Third parties set the reimbursement rates, and patients are usually not even aware of the cost of their healthcare." If health care were a commodity, we would see greater competition among providers to bring down the cost of care. In fact, we find the complete opposite to be true, with often vastly different prices for the same quality of services, often within the same region.[153]

Defining health as a commodity is incorrect and immoral. Not only does it contradict our fundamental right to life, but it makes the false assumption that the quality of health care is no different, regardless of how it is provided. Furthermore, it keeps us arguing about the role of government, while our health and budget continue to deteriorate. Every American should be entitled to adequate quality health care. By acknowledging health as right, we can get down to the important business of reducing its cost, in the interest of the patient alone. Universal health care does not mean rationed care. If we actually spent our energy trying to cut waste from the system, we could guarantee better health care for all with a much greater choice of providers. Our economy would be far better off and we would not be forced to choose between life and death for many of our citizens.

Quality and Accountability

CONTROLLING THE QUALITY AND ACCOUNTABILITY OF care will be crucial to the success of the co-op. Our current health care system lacks the proper mechanisms to monitor and standardize specific measurements of good care. It allows profit, rather than expert, unbiased, professional opinions and patient feedback to dictate the priorities of our doctors and other care providers. The present mechanism to ensure accountability for the quality of care given to patients is insufficient.

The co-op will address these issues by setting up a peer evaluation system for doctors and other health providers. Additionally, the co-op will cover the cost of malpractice judgments and settlements directly, and monitor all contracts with individual providers. The co-op will conduct a quarterly process of self-auditing to publicize its budgetary data. These measures will improve care, ensure transparency, and bring down cost.

Malpractice Reform

The co-op will use its contingency fund, generated by policyholder premiums, to pay malpractice awards, legal fees, and settlements on behalf of its doctors and other health providers. Doctors will no longer feel obligated to practice defensive medicine by ordering unnecessary tests and invasive diagnostic procedures—a common strategy to avoid malpractice in for-profit medicine. Moreover, by covering malpractice settlements, the health care provider takes responsibility for the performance of its doctors, creating an internal quality control incentive within the co-op. In the current system, the insurance, provider network, and drug and device companies do not set responsible incentives to prevent malpractice. Furthermore, they use doctors as the foot soldiers of abuse.

To provide anonymity in malpractice cases, the co-op will assign codes to all individual doctors. Provider identity will remain confidential except at the highest level of management, which may require specific identities in order to judge and settle claims. Doctors and other providers must be prepared to explain their cases to the courts, as per normal malpractice procedures. As the co-op will provide care at much lower costs, settlements will be lower than the current average, but payouts will be sufficient to provide wrongfully treated policyholders with adequate compensation.

Transparency

Each year, third party accountants will audit the co-op. The accountants shall have no conflicts of interests in performing their function. The accounting firms will change periodically every two years to prevent the development of biases and conflicts of interest between the auditing agencies and the co-op's upper-management. Audits will be posted on the co-op's website, so that the public may judge the authenticity and integrity of the organization's finances. Access to results will be available to all co-op members, as well as government and employer contractors.

Incentivizing Quality Care

To eliminate the vast array of unethical medical practices that arise from our for-profit health care system, we must change doctors' incentives. They must be properly rewarded for prioritizing high quality care over all other motivations.

As a preventive measure, doctors employed by the co-op will be required to divest themselves of all conflicts of interest with the for-profit health care industry. This divestment will be completely mandatory and strictly enforced. Those concealing conflicts will be removed immediately from their positions at the co-op and may have to pay a fine, depending on the severity of the case. A robust enforcement mechanism will serve to identify and reprimand those who violate this important contractual stipulation.

To incentivize doctors towards the best practices, the co-op will award bonuses based on comprehensive doctor evaluations that include input from both patients and peers. Patients receiving co-op services will regularly complete anonymous satisfaction reports on the quality of care provided by their doctor. All doctors contracted by the co-op will conduct performance reviews of their peers. To guarantee objectivity, the reviewer will be anonymous to the identity of the reviewed. The co-op will assign identification numbers to doctors, nurses, and other service providers to ensure impartiality throughout the review process. Evaluations will be based on current standard of care guidelines. All providers will spend part of their time as evaluators, conducting a steady but relatively small amount of peer review.

Quarterly peer review scores will be combined with patient satisfaction reports to create a final evaluation score on a scale of 1 to 100. This rating will serve as the basis for retention, demotion, and bonuses. If a provider performs average care—a year end average score between 65 and 85—he or she will receive normal compensation. If the provider scores above 85, he or she will receive a bonus, on an annual basis. In no case, should the bonus exceed double the provider's annual salary. If a provider scores below 65, their compensation will be cut. Scores below 50 during any quarter will result in probation and mandatory retraining. A consistent annual score below 50 will result in dismissal. The exact cutoff points for these standards are subject to change with experience. Bonuses will be funded by an extra charge of one quarter of one percent on all policy holders, included in the price of the health policy. Given an estimated annual policy price of $4,000—more than half the current cost per patient on Medicare and Medicaid—the extra annual charge per policy will be equivalent to $10. A co-op with 120 million policy holders will generate $1.2 billion, in additional employee and management income to incentivize the best quality care.

How to Save a Trillion Dollars

IN OUR LAST HEALTH CARE DEBATE, MANY FEARED THAT the only way to reduce costs was to ration care or increase government spending. We spent very little time discussing how to improve the treatment decisions made by our doctors. Given the tremendous cost of unnecessary surgeries, redundant tests, and prolonged treatments, we have the potential to realize massive savings through minor changes in doctor's incentives. By basing compensation on peer and patient evaluations, rather than on maximizing revenue or minimizing costs, the co-op will provide better care for less money.

Beyond improving the fundamental incentives that define our health care delivery system, the co-op will also address hundreds of billions in administrative waste. The co-op will save money in five ways:

1) Reduce billing expenses to a fraction of present costs
2) Eliminate opportunities for fraudulent billing by consolidating the payment system
3) Reduce provider overhead by covering administrative costs through the co-op,
4) Eliminate unnecessary tests, drugs, and procedures by removing the profit motive from the provider

5) Lower the price of equipment, drugs and devices by negotiating bulk prices with the pharmaceutical industry and other vendors.

Administrative Savings

Our plan for nonprofit health care will eliminate waste by consolidating the inefficient mess of provider overhead. Every year, the US health care system spends $650 billion on administrative costs alone, the highest health related administrative costs in the world. Our doctors spend about 27 percent of their gross income on these costs.[154] Just to execute basic billing functions, doctors must hire coding specialists whose sole responsibility consists of determining how to charge insurance companies for services. Coder salaries often surpass $43,000 per year, as many receive bonuses based on the amount that they are able to bill.[155] By eliminating coding and other billing costs, and contracting directly with realtors and hospitals for practice space, the co-op will relieve doctors of their administrative expenditures and duties. By saving money and time on overhead and administration, the co-op will be able to afford higher salaries for its doctors, and patients will receive more time and attention from their care providers.

Health without Fraud

Consolidated billing will drastically reduce fraud costs. The government estimates fraud committed each year at $98 billion, but the actual amount is closer to $196 billion.[156] Furthermore, we have to acknowledge that many minor instances of fraud used to maximize income go undetected, but probably add up to unknown billions of dollars. Over the course of 40 years of experience as an insider, I have personally observed countless instances of blatant fraud and overuse. Several billion more are wasted, just in the process of uncovering, investigating, and prosecuting cases.

Patient Savings

Patients covered under the co-op will pay much less for their policies, while receiving just the right amount of quality care. A basic policy with the co-op will cost about $4,000 per year. This figure is about half the average cost of those now covered by Medicaid and Medicare.

Under the co-op program, the amount of money saved on Medicare and Medicaid will be enough to cover costs for all our senior citizens, without co-pays, deductibles or fees for essential medication and devices. Seniors will be free to use their hard-earned savings to enjoy their retirement or pass something on to their descendants. By eliminating co-pay, the only expense for seniors or other policyholders will be a small $25 charge for initiating appointments. Co-op members will save substantial out-of-pocket money and enjoy trustworthy, good quality care. Additionally, and most importantly, they will gain a voice by evaluating the quality of care they receive. They are in a position to choose and reward their caregivers.

Doctor's Savings

These days, doctors finish medical school with significant debt, and usually without the resources to establish their own practices. The average medical student graduates with a debt burden of about $160,000.[157] With interest over time, the student ends up paying $600,000.[158] Due to the high cost of setting up a private practice, two-thirds of all doctors end up working for a partnership, hospital, HMO, or under several IPA or PPO contracts.[159] The co-op will offer doctors a career option superior to the current health care industry standard. For the first time in decades, doctors will be free from the logistics of running a business, worrying about malpractice, and dealing with a disorganized billing system. Doctors will only be expected to treat a reasonable number of patients and will not need to moonlight in emergency rooms to support themselves and their families, as many under HMO contracts do now. They will be free to focus exclusively on the needs of their patients and will be directly rewarded by these merits alone. The coop will provide doctors with a deal superior to any option in our current for-profit system, by offering a salary at 25 percent above the current market rate.

Government Savings

Not only will savings from the co-op benefit patients and doctors, they will reduce our government's budget deficit. By transferring all patients covered under Medicare and Medicaid into the cost saving co-op, the government will succeed in reforming some of its most expensive entitlement programs. Our senior population is rising faster than any other demographic group.[160] If we do not figure out how to control the inevitable rise in health care costs to support them, we will end up bankrupting our economy or sacrificing our seniors. Fortunately, the co-op will reduce costs in half, while providing a higher level of treatment. Our health care plan amounts to not only savings without cuts, while providing comprehensive care at a higher quality.

The co-op will save the federal government between $391 and $456 billion each year. At present, public spending accounts for 46 percent of all health care spending in the United States.[161] According to former US Comptroller General, David Walker, if increases in the cost of Medicare and Medicaid continue on its present course, by 2050 the federal government will spend $14 trillion on Medicare and Medicaid programs alone, or nearly $14,000 per household.[162] While initial expenditures are necessary to establish the infrastructure to manage this influx in patients, over the long run, our Medicare and Medicaid costs will plummet to a fraction of their current price. This initial setup cost may be provided by government loans now available to nonprofit health insurance companies, available as per the ACA. This provision may be extended to the nonprofit co-op health care provider, and paid back amortized to the life of the loan. Excluding the difficult process of measuring savings from negotiating bulk prices, the co-op will save the government hundreds of billions of dollars in the following four categories:

Direct savings from consolidating billing costs: $55 billion
Savings from fraud reduction: $60–125 billion
Savings from overhead reduction: $53.4 billion
Savings from eliminating unnecessary tests, drugs, and procedures: $247.8 billion

Total federal savings: $420–480 billion per year

Bulk Price Negotiation Savings

The co-op will leverage its large customer base to purchase bulk goods and services at a discount. Medicare and Medicaid together contract with 119 million people, a number roughly equal to the entire population of Mexico.[163] With one entity purchasing services and products for more than 119 million policyholders, the co-op will be in a strong position to negotiate bulk prices with the pharmaceutical and biotech industries. Pharmaceutical companies have previously lobbied to forbid the government from engaging in these types of negotiations. But, since the co-op will be an independent, private corporation, it will be free to negotiate with drug and device companies, as well as other service providers. Furthermore, it will be free from the influence of industry lobbyists, as the co-op doctors and managers responsible for negotiating contracts will be barred from holding financial stakes in outside entities providing goods or services to the co-op. The co-op will channel the collective negotiating power of hundreds of millions of consumers, rather than allowing them to remain dispersed and unrepresented in our current fragmented system.

For the pharmaceutical industry, the days of 30 percent profit margins may be over. To survive, drug companies will be forced to innovate, rather than spend their money marketing and lobbying minor improvements on existing drugs. The co-op will only purchase equipment and drugs based on their contribution to patient health and as a result, pharmaceutical companies will be pressured to prioritize the development of useful drugs. By changing the incentives of providers towards better health and eliminating the professional conflict of interest, the co-op will indirectly improve the pharmaceutical industry.

Patient Choice and Freedom

THE CO-OP WILL FREE PATIENTS FROM THE BURDEN OF HIGH insurance premiums and harmful surgeries, while offering a larger array of services than any other current provider. Patients will still have the freedom to buy other forms of insurance. However, the co-op's network of physicians and specialists will be nearly six times larger than any existing health management plan. Opting for a policy covered by the co-op will provide patients with a significantly greater choice in physicians and specialists.

Over the last decade, the managed care option has emerged as a dominant model of health care distribution in the United States. In 2000, HMOs and PPOs contracted with 43 percent of doctors. Today, nearly 64 percent of doctors contract with these management networks. Patients covered by these plans agree to visit only certain doctors and hospitals within the network. In exchange, the network acts as a middleman by managing doctors' fees or salaries and setting their incentives.

In its current state, managed care systems tend to limit patient choice. Patients who contract with an HMO cannot select providers outside their designated network. Additionally, all of their care is managed by a primary care physician who makes decisions on their behalf. Under PPOs, patients have the option to seek physicians outside the network, but at a much greater cost.

In the early 1990s, health insurers and employers launched a major effort to limits options covered by manage care. The effort placed further restrictions on the number of specialists and hospitals available to patients, causing a major consumer backlash. As resistance to the restrictions imposed by managed care gained force, prominent politicians came to their defense, advocating in support of "patient choice." Ultimately, most managed care organizations decided to reconsider their restrictions.[164] Nonetheless, the basic framework of HMOs and PPOs remained in place and patient choice remains very limited to this day. HMOs still limit patients to services within their network, while PPOs exact penalties for selecting physicians outside the network.

Under the proposed co-op, patients will have more choice than they presently do in either HMO or PPO programs. Because the co-op will contract with the government to cover those under Medicare, Medicaid, and SCHIP, the co-op program will begin with at least 119 million policyholders. The co-op provider network will be nearly a dozen times larger than Kaiser, offering patients a more flexible array of doctors and hospitals. Rather than establishing an exclusive enclave of doctors and specialists, like most HMOs, IPAs, and PPOs, the co-op will consolidate a giant network of diverse professionals.

The national co-op will also provide both employers and employees with low cost comprehensive policies, allowing them more flexibility. By offering an affordable option to our workers, the co-op will help eliminate "job lock," an inefficiency that occurs when employees stay with jobs solely for the purpose of retaining their health care benefits. Eliminating job lock will grant patients the freedom to pursue work anywhere, without fear of losing their health care coverage. One study conducted at UC Berkeley, found that job lock accounts for $772 million in lost productivity each year in California alone.[165] Under the co-op, employers will find it easier to transfer policies. Since individuals will be able to move anywhere in the country without changing plans, our workforce will be better equipped to respond to the constantly evolving structure of our economy.

A healthier and more productive workforce will produce enormous residual benefits for the entire economy. Lower worker productivity brought on by poor health from a lack of health insurance, results in an economic loss of $225.8 billion each year or about $1,685 for every employee in the US.[166] By mitigating this loss, the co-op will actually increase the size of our economy by a quarter of a trillion dollars. Additionally, business tax incentives will remain in place, with employee health care classified as a deductible expense. Expanded employee health coverage through the affordable co-op, will further increase deductions. As the co-op is nonprofit and recognizes the patient as the primary stakeholder, all surplus revenue will be returned to policy purchasers, including individual employers and the government. Rather than paying dividends to large and often disinterested financial stakeholders, the co-op will compensate the most important parties from within the cooperative organization.

The cooperative care model will cut more than a trillion and a half in waste, eliminate harmful conflicts of interest, expand our economy, and provide our citizens with better care. In this health maximizing system, we the people emerge as the sole motivation of doctors, hospitals, and clinics. While many argue that the government has no constitutional obligation to provide health care entitlements for all, doing so is essential to guaranteeing our right to life, liberty, and the pursuit of happiness. So far, we have approached the issue from the wrong angle. When we have so much space to eliminate waste, increasing government spending is not the solution. Though troubling, the massive amount of fraud and waste in the health care industry presents us with an extraordinary opportunity to achieve our nation's full potential. If implemented, the proposed co-op plan will reduce health care costs to just 8 percent of our GDP, freeing up the other 92 percent to reduce our debt and invest in a prosperous future.

The cooperative care model represents the only fully nonprofit health care system within the private sector. The next and final section of the book explores various international health care models for comparison.

GLOBAL PERSPECTIVE

Better Care, Lower Cost

The United States of America is the most powerful, most innovative, and richest nation the planet has ever known. [But,] when it comes to the essential task of providing health care for people, the mighty USA is a fourth-rate power.
- T.R. Reid, *The Healing of America.*[167]

OUR HEALTH CARE SYSTEM HAS MANY STRONG DEFENDERS. In an interview with CBS' Face the Nation, House Majority Leader John Boehner declared that "Obamacare will bankrupt our country and ruin the best health care delivery system in the world." Senate Minority Leader Mitch McConnell, R-Ky, reiterated Boehner's view, calling our health care "the finest health care system in the world."[168] Despite their noble defense of American pride, these politicians have either taken liberties with fact or have been seriously misinformed.

Those supporting the notion that we have the world's best health care system often cite the number of foreigners who come to the US for special treatments. Michael Tanner, a scholar at the CATO institute noted, "whether the disease is cancer, pneumonia, heart disease or AIDS, the chances of a patient surviving are far higher in the US than in other countries." He cited instances in which foreign celebrities and politicians opted to seek intensive care in the US, rather than their home countries.[169] To Tanner's credit, we may lead the way on a number of complicated procedures, given our technological and financial resources, but in the vast majority of cases, the US offers inferior care at a premium price.

As T.R. Reid argues in his book, *The Healing of America*, "for anyone with the money—or the insurance policy—to pay for it, American medical treatment ranks with the best on earth. That's why seriously rich people all over the world tend to board their private jets and race to some famous American clinic when they face a medical emergency." However, the high cost of health care in United States cripples its ability to offer meaningful care for tens of millions of its own citizens.[170]

According to the WHO, the US health care system ranks 37th, just behind Costa Rica and eight countries behind Morocco. Last formulated in 2000, this measure, although controversial, was the only one to compare performance with price to provide a comprehensive score. Though the US provided the 15th highest quality of care, we paid more per capita than any other country.[171] In 2009, the average US citizen paid $7,960, while Canadians paid $4,314, Germans paid $4,219, the French paid $3,969, the British paid $3,438, and Israelis paid $2,111.[172] For a fraction of the price, our international counterparts in developed countries receive better care.

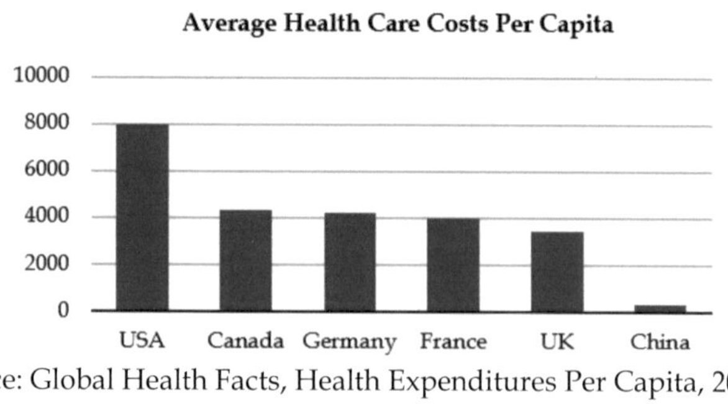

Source: Global Health Facts, Health Expenditures Per Capita, 2009.[173]

Compared with 34 developed countries, the US ranks 31st at preventing infant mortality (behind Poland and Slovakia), 31st in ensuring access to health care (25 developed countries insure 99 percent of citizens), 27th in extending life expectancy (behind Slovenia and Chile), and 29th in the number of practicing doctors per patient (2.4 per 1,000 people, compared with an average of 3.1 in other developed countries). Unsurprisingly, the US has the highest instance of unmet care due to cost, when compared with 11 developed countries surveyed on this category. Thirty-nine percent of the US population living below the average income, and 20 percent of those above-average income, chose to forego doctors' visits and prescriptions on account of the high cost.[174]

Illustrative of our poor health performance, the TV show 20/20 ran a special on infant mortality in Memphis, Tennessee, called "Babyland." The show featured a small corner of the city's public cemetery dubbed by locals as Babyland and used to bury the babies of low income mothers. In 2006 alone, 202 babies died in Memphis – almost four every week – nearly double the 122 people murdered in the same year [176.[175]

The argument in defense of our health care system is both incorrect and irresponsible. We fail to deliver on a number of our country's crucial health needs and by denying responsibility we allow the problem to persist. While admitting our poor health performance among countries of similar economic prosperity may be painful, we have much to gain from the perspective. By learning from the advantages and failings of other health care systems across the world, we can best address our own.

Canada

ALL CANADIANS ARE COVERED THROUGH A COMBINATION of private insurance and a government payment program also known as Medicare. Two-thirds of Canadians purchase private insurance and the rest opt for Medicare. Private insurance covers dental, prescription drugs, and in home care. The Canadian system is not socialized medicine.[176] Though the government pays the health provider directly, all services come from the private sector. This arrangement costs the average Canadian about $4,314 each year, or nearly half the price paid in the US. Even at a lower cost, 84.4 percent of Canadians said they were "very satisfied" or "somewhat satisfied" with their health services. Most savings come from a consolidated billing process that eliminates complicated payment agreements. Other savings come from the industry's ability to leverage its concentrated consumer base to negotiate bulk prices for drugs and devices.[177]

Canadian health care is financed by three main sources. 1) Medicare, which finances 70 percent of health care costs, draws its funding from general taxation. 2) Out-of-pocket payments by individuals and 3) private insurance, together, account for the other 30 percent of health care financing.

Doctors at hospitals and in private practice bill using a fee-for-service model. Hospitals are almost all nonprofit and owned by religious orders, universities, governments, and municipalities. Though a for-profit option exists, it is generally cheaper than nonprofit care, but offers a lower staff-to-patient ratio.

Canada's centralized funding evolved in tandem with a decentralized model. Before 1957, the provinces paid for all health care coverage. In that year, the federal government set up a new agreement to pay for half of all costs through a matching system. The federal government's commitment led to expanded coverage, but also raised spending and increased patient wait time. To curb costs, the federal government has since decreased its commitment to cover just 25 percent of provincial health care costs. Though a quarter of the funding comes from the federal government, the individual provinces set standards and manage their own health care system. This decentralized model, allows each province to tailor its health care system to meet its unique health needs.

In 1966, the federal government nationalized health care under the Medical Care Insurance Act. The effect created near universal coverage for office and clinic based physician care and diagnostic services. This act was in part a response to earlier legislation passed in Saskatchewan in 1962, which provided universal coverage for physician services in the province. In response, the physicians went on strike, leading to a compromise, whereby they were given the option to charge patients above the fee set by the government. At first, 12 percent of doctors over-billed to make up for the difference in lost income, but by 1974 only 2 percent did so, due to market pressures that increased the basic cost of care. However, the extra revenue from increasingly expensive treatments went directly to the doctors, rather than accruing in the hands of insurance companies and drug and device manufactures.

Canada's biggest hurdles are rising expenses, an aging population, and wait time. That said, much of the criticism of Canada's wait time is a myth, or at least deserves to be put in broader context. One study showed that in Canada, the wait time was about four weeks for elective surgery and four weeks for diagnostic tests. By comparison, in the US, 32 percent of patients waited more than a month for elective surgery, and 5 percent waited more than four months.

Canada's health care system benefits from being mostly nonprofit. In instances in which profit does become a factor, it does not accrue with peripheral stakeholders in drug, device, and insurance companies. The benefits of profit directly affect physicians, providing some indirect monetary incentives to those closest to the patient. Canada's health care structure is also highly adaptable. Its matching program provides centralized funding, while still allowing provinces the freedom to address their own health needs. [178]

China

CHINA'S UNIVERSAL HEALTH CARE SYSTEM IS COMPLICATED by the county's struggle to control urbanization and internal migration. Interestingly, it suffers from many of the same problem of insufficient coverage and poor quality faced by the United States, although on a much larger scale.[179] Though 95 percent of Chinese citizens are insured, at least nominally by the government, the system excludes more than 225 million farmworkers who have migrated to the cities.[180] In China, access to social services is tied to the location of one's birth. In order to regulate the movement of hundreds of millions of people over millennia, China requires internal migrants to pay for services offered in their new homes. While this law has mitigated the overstrain on resources in the cities, it has left nearly a quarter of a billion people without insurance or access to health care. Access is also limited by the payment structure. Hospital expenses are reimbursed only after the patient has covered all costs, restricting access for people who cannot afford to pay for the treatment up front. On the other hand, this method makes patients aware of the true costs, reducing fraud, abuse, and over-billing.[181]

The profound divide between the rural and urban populations characterizes the structure of China's health care system. The government splits coverage options between rural citizens, classified by the grouping R and consisting of 54.3 percent of the population and urban citizens, classified by the grouping U and consisting of 45.7 percent of the population. The U group is covered by employer-based insurance. Eighty-six percent of rural residents categorized under the R group received coverage from the "New Cooperative Medical Scheme." For the U group, government-owned city hospitals constitute the majority of urban care. Hospitals borrow from state banks to purchase high-tech medical devices and expand facilities, but because the hospitals are state-owned they are virtually exempt from foreclosure. As a result, hospitals accrue huge amounts of debt.

Though the government owns most major urban hospitals, overall ownership of health facilities is fairly diverse. According to the Chinese Ministry of Health, 31 percent of health care institutions are owned by the state, 47 percent by private companies, 15 percent by people's cooperatives, and 7 percent by other arrangements.

To regulate the industry, the Chinese government attempts to control the price of drugs. However, its effort is largely unsuccessful, as pharmaceutical companies tend to avert restrictions by renaming and repackaging their drugs. From 1998 to 2006, the government implemented 17 unsuccessful price reductions.

Funding for China's health care system originates from three sources: government, enterprise, and individuals. The government covers the cost through taxation and fees charged on each provider. Local taxation and fees fund each province's health care system, resulting in disparity of care between rich regions and poor regions. The government pressures private enterprise to insure all its employees. Out-of-pocket payments made by individuals helps bridge the gap between what the government is able to provide and the necessary level of care.

Over the last three decades, a number of reforms have shifted the bulk of payment responsibility onto the individual and away from the government. From 1980 to 2007, direct government expenditures dropped from 36.2 percent to 20.3 percent of total health care spending. Over the same time period, spending on health care for the poor dropped from 52.6 percent to 34.5 percent, while private out-of-pocket expenditure climbed from 21.2 percent to 45.2 percent. This trend may lead to increased disparity in quality of care and a growing burden among impoverished individuals to pay directly for care.

It is a tradition in Chinese medical practice for patients to pay doctors a very large tip, known as "red-envelope money," to ensure good service. Doctors also earn extra revenue from commissions on their drug sales. Though to a certain extent "red envelope money" provides doctors with incentive to provide better care for their patients, doctors are also encouraged by pharmaceutical companies to prescribe certain drugs, regardless of their potential benefits. Moreover, the status quo practice of tipping, often encourages doctors to skimp on care for those who have not paid extra.

Hospitals are subsidized by the government to cover the cost of its facilities, but have some freedom to pursue money-making ventures outside the public interest. Because hospitals are neither privately owned nor profit-maximizing, they end up pursuing primarily staff interests. As the government regulates treatment costs, but cannot control the price of drugs, hospitals make up the difference by providing treatments at a fixed price. Doing so minimizes quality and maximizes pharmaceutical commissions. The government is now considering whether to invite foreign capital to city hospitals, with a stipulation that caps foreign ownership at 70 percent.

In 1965, Chairman Mao Zedong implemented a number of public health programs, as part of the Cultural Revolution.[182] Upon taking power in 1949, the Communist Party faced the challenge of providing health for a population of 540 million, with just 40,000 physicians trained in western medical practices. Given the small ratio of health care professionals to patients, the People's Republic of China had to rely on millions of paramedical auxiliaries, known as "bare-foot doctors." With little training, they were nonetheless able to provide vaccinations, antibiotics, and education to hundreds of millions living at the subsistence level. An extensive program of rural health clinics helped provide the country's impoverished masses with some form of basic care for the first time. Between the revolution and 1980, life expectancy increased by 25 years, the most rapid improvement ever documented for a country this size.

China's health care system changed dramatically with the free market reforms of Deng Xiaoping. Urban health centers remained largely state-owned, but rural clinics were either disbanded or placed under private ownership.[183] In the late 1980s, the Chinese government launched health care reform initiatives, transferring responsibility for financing and administration from the central government to the provinces. The drop in coverage that accompanied these reforms has caused the Chinese public to regard them as highly unsuccessful.

In 1997, additional reforms changed the financing schemes of many hospitals away from an expensive pay-for-service model. In the new arrangement, 90 percent of hospital funding would be based on expenditures from the previous year, with the remaining 10 percent dependent on the quality of care. The payment scheme succeeded in limiting rises in cost by curbing the over prescription of expensive drugs and procedures. However, delivery continues to suffer from institutional inefficiency.

Though past reforms may have favored the urban population, recent government commitments have benefited the entire health care system. Between 2006 and 2007, the government increased its health care spending by 87 percent to address insufficient coverage. The Chinese health care system continues to struggle with cost inflation and insufficient coverage. As urbanization continues, the government must balance the health needs of rural migrants with the strained resources of its growing cities. Moreover, the aging population will need significant care in the future. Given the one child policy, family contributions will be insufficient to care for both parents.

France

ALL FRENCH CITIZENS ARE ENTITLED TO NATIONAL HEALTH insurance, which pays for hospitals, ambulances, and prescription drugs, with some dental care included. Public funds cover 78 percent of health care costs. The remainder is paid by employers and a tiny fraction covered by the employee. Public funding comes from a combination of payroll taxes, contributions from other social security programs, tobacco and alcohol taxes, and state subsidies. Though the government pays the health providers, many operate in the private sector. Two-thirds of hospital beds are public or nonprofit, with salaried physicians. One-third of hospital beds are for-profit, with physicians paid on a fee-for-service basis. Ninety-two percent of patients are permitted to buy private insurance, in addition to the national insurance option. While all services covered by the public option require cost-sharing arrangements with the patient's employer, these requirements are waived for those suffering from any of 32 specified chronic diseases, as well as the poor.

In 2000, the WHO ranked France's health care system the best in the world. High quality care, combined with significant coverage at a low cost to the patient, makes the French system inclusive and effective. A study conducted in 2008, by the US Journal of Health Affairs, found that from 2002 to 2003, France had the lowest death rate for ailments treatable with basic care.[184] By contrast, the US ranked 19th globally. The French utilize more health care than Americans, averaging six physician visits each year, compared with less than three in the United States. The average French citizen pays only $3,969 per year, half the price of US care.[185] Overall, the US spends 17.8 percent of its GDP on health care, while France spends just 11.8 percent.

The establishment of a robust social security program, allowed for France's publicly funded health care model. Following World War II, France founded a large social security program known as Sécurité Sociale, which in respect to health care, emphasized a private fee-for-service model, but agreed to reimburse patients for 80 percent of costs.[186] Initially, doctors objected to the prices set by the government. However, in 1960, President Charles de Gaulle pressured the health care industry to accept the payment changes, famously stating, "I saved France on a colonel's salary." Eventually, doctors embraced the program for the sake of guaranteeing a steady supply of patients.

Today, patients still pay physicians directly, before reimbursement by Sécurité Sociale. The direct billing method allows patients to better monitor the fees charged for each treatment or procedure, while reimbursement guarantees its affordability. Direct payment also functions as a cost control mechanism, a simple solution absent in the US where insurance companies and the government pay doctors without patient knowledge.

The French system incentivizes doctors to provide high quality care and reduces the conflict of interest that develops when the health delivery system prioritizes the profit motive. In 2009, the public health insurance scheme launched an incentive program, known as the Individual Practice Improvement Contract (CAPI).[187] The program tied monetary rewards of up to €5,000 to targets in the care for asthma, diabetes, hypertension, immunization, and breast cancer screening. The contracts also stipulated the prescription of generic drugs over more expensive name brands, especially for cardiovascular conditions. Initially, resistance from physicians' unions and the pharmaceutical industry contested these changes. However, soon after implementation, providers adopted the new rules without any significant problems.

With an aging population and the development of new expensive treatments, cost control remains an important issue for the French government. Additionally, the French health care system must work on improving efficiency through a national computerized system of medical records to reduce overprescription. Overall, France represents a partial, but significant success in the tug of war between profit and quality care.

Germany

THE GERMAN HEALTH CARE MODEL OFFERS AN EXEMPLARY case for the effectiveness of a robust nonprofit option in the private sector. Germany provides health for 92 percent of its population through hundreds of private nonprofit insurance companies, known as Krankenkassen or "sickness funds."[188] As health is guaranteed by the constitution, the government requires the Krankenkassen to provide full coverage to all applicants. Though heavily regulated and nonprofit, the Krankenkassen engage in a competitive market, stimulating improvements in quality without incentives to deny or preference certain clients. The controlled competition bars insurance companies from selecting customers based on their risk profiles. Instead, insurers compete by matching services to fit the needs of the customer's income level.[189] To manage competition, the government divides the consumer market into two income levels. Nonprofit insurance companies are permitted to charge 8.2 percent of annual income on policy holders earning less than €50,850 a year. The employer then pays an additional 7.3 percent. Those earning above €50,850, may opt out of the Krankenkassen to purchase private insurance.[190] In reality, only 8 percent choose outside plans.[191]

Insurance companies negotiate contracts with health providers for services. Certified health providers may establish their own practice or take a salaried position at any hospital or provider organization in the private and public sector. Private companies own half of hospitals, while the rest remain public. The vast majority of doctors are salaried. The owners of the hospitals and clinics bill the insurer for each service provided.

Every year, health care costs the German economy 11.6 percent of GDP or about $4,218 per capita, roughly 30 percent more than the developed country average, but significantly less than the United States.[192] Germany has one of the world's lowest infant mortality rates at 3.5 deaths per 1,000 live births and is tied for the fourth lowest mortality rate for those under the age of five.[193] The average German lives to 83-years-old, only surpassed by eight other countries. However, longer lives have driven up the cost of health care, from just 8 percent of GDP in 1995. As one in five Germans is over the age of 65—one of the highest percentage of seniors in the world—caring for the elderly has become an immense challenge for the health care delivery system.[194] Over the next decades, the country's GDP growth will struggle to compensate for the rising cost of health care, as fewer young people enter the workforce, compared with those departing.

Germany has a long tradition of ensuring health for its citizens. In the 1890s, Chancellor Otto von Bismarck established a number of insurance programs to cover the health of workers and the elderly. Following World War II, the health care system split in two. In West Germany, the government mandated insurance and supervised the practices of the mostly private health care industry. During the mid-1980s and 1990s, the government reformed the system to allow for greater patient choice and industry competition. The changes, transformed health care from a supply side delivery model to a demand based system. In line with its Soviet jurisdiction, East Germany adopted a completely government run health care system, from insurance to providers. Upon reunification, East Germany took on the West German model. Since then, health care reform has aimed at unifying the two systems.

The German system offers an interesting combination of public regulation and private choice. By controlling the incentives of insurance competition, the government optimizes the industry in the direct interest of the patient, rather than the company. Salaried doctors reduce conflicting financial interests and ensure quality care. The German system protects patients from exploitation, while taking advantage of the efficiencies of the free market. However, the large influx in retirees may make the current system unsustainable over the next few decades.

United Kingdom

THE UNITED KINGDOM PROVIDES UNIVERSAL COVERAGE through A socialized system, known as the National Health Service (NHS), which pays health care providers directly. The NHS covers 90 percent of UK citizens for hospital, ambulatory, and physician services, as well as prescription drugs, with all care free at the point of service. The NHS pays for 86 percent of health costs with 11.9 percent matched by patients and the rest paid solely by patients opting for private sector coverage.[195] Just 10 percent of the population choose private care, which offers more provider options and less wait time for elective surgery.

Most practitioners are paid directly by the state and managed through standards and compensation set by 152 Primary Care Trusts (PCTs), which control 80 percent of the UK's health budget. Primary care providers are private, but contract directly with PCTs through a mix of salary, capitation, and fee-for-service. Physicians are incentivized by PCT contracts to hit certain health performance targets, with a portion of income dependent on quality and innovation. Each practice is scored on 146 performance indicators, with about 18 percent of practice earnings dependent on achievement.[196]

In 1946, Parliament established the NHS to provide broad coverage for its citizens unable to afford out-of-pocket care. The effect nationalized the hospital system and universalized coverage. Today, the NHS is the single largest employer in England, with around 1.3 million employees. Britons consider the right to free health care an important aspect of citizenship and express satisfaction for the state-run system. Due to its centralized nature, the British health care system makes it easy for the entire industry to adopt standards and advancements in delivery. Since 2002, the government has implemented a nationwide health information network to share important information across the system.

Though expensive advances in treatment combined with caring for a growing population of retirees continues to inflate costs, the average UK citizen pays just $3,438 each year, less than half the amount charged in the US.[197] For their money, Britons are 30 percent more likely to survive through the first year of life and on average, live one year longer than their American counterparts.[198] Additionally, British citizens suffer from lower rates of diabetes, heart attack, stroke, lung disease, cancer, hypertension, and heart disease.[199] Controlling cost increases remains a concern, but recent developments may be indicative of an affordable future. From 1997 to 2010, health care costs as a percentage of GDP rose from 6.6 percent to 9.7 percent. However, between 2009 and 2010 this cost actually fell by about 1 percent. In this particular instance, savings came from the public sector, while private sector costs still increased by 1.6 percent as a percentage of GDP. Much of the drop resulted from an economic recovery of 4.6 percent in 2010, compared with an economic contraction of 2.8 percent, in 2009.[200]

The British health care system benefits from consistency, simplicity, and incentives that encourage doctors to meet health based targets. Though choice of coverage is limited by the universal system, a private insurance option exists for those able to afford it. The balance of private and public sector costs over the next few years may be instructive of the system's long-term viability.

A Plan for Health and Prosperity

THOUGH NOT WITHOUT THEIR FAULTS, MANY OF THESE INternational health care models offer better care than our own and at a fraction of the price. The Canadian system benefits from its adaptability to local needs; the German system represents a robust example of nonprofit private sector insurance; France administers a partnership between a strong social security network and a highly qualified staff of private doctors; and the UK shows the viability and affordability of a government run system with a private sector option. Most importantly, regardless of how each health care system is set up, all offer some form of incentive for doctors to provide better health. On the other hand, China offers a surprising point of comparison with the failings of limited access and high cost present in our own health care system.

However, with the exception of the German model, none of these systems combine the efficiencies of the private sector with the need to eliminate the profit motive from our health. Most of these models prefer to use government as the only nonprofit entity. Placing the state as the largest provider or insurer has the potential to insulate the system in bureaucratic management. In many cases, this model can discourage innovation and limit patient choice. By contrast, the cooperative care model described in this book takes a reverse approach. Rather than using the government as the primary insurer, the proposed co-op will insure the government, covering all policies under Medicare, Medicaid, and SHICP.

We need a fully nonprofit option within the private sector that is strong enough to administer all aspects of health care, from insurance to check ups, medications, and surgeries. No other country offers such a comprehensive private sector plan capable of removing the profit motive completely at the point of service of the health care delivery system. In order to truly optimize our nation's health, we must make sure that every segment of our health delivery system places patient needs as its only priority. The cooperative care model makes our doctors trustworthy and accountable, while encouraging them to offer the highest level of care, regardless of the patient's income level or preexisting conditions. This nonprofit model seeks to bring our money into the service of good health.

By expanding the ACA's nonprofit insurance company into a private nonprofit health care provider, we will finally be able to realize tremendous savings in money and lives. Setting up the co-op will take significant political courage and economic investment. However, once we have made the initial investment, we will see returns in good health for decades to come. With massive health care legislation about to be implemented, we are better poised than ever to enact the best possible solution. Doing so will help us face one of the greatest challenges of our time. A comprehensive, private nonprofit health care option will stunt our mounting deficit and slash our debt, while establishing good health as our right to life, liberty, and the pursuit of happiness. The co-op will save more than a trillion dollars every year, increase productivity through better health, and grant our households and corporations extra money to pursue other important priorities. Simply put, this proposed health care plan is a plan for a prosperous American future—a future of good health, freedom, and personal enrichment.

References

[1] Biley, Francis C. "The 'Sickening' Search for Health: Ivan Illich's Revised Thoughts on the Medicalization of Life and Medical Iatrogenesis." *International Journal of Holistic Healing* 10 no. 2, (May, 2010). http://ip-72-167-195-46.ip.secureserver.net/user_files/documents/ijhc/articles/Biley-10-2F.pdf.

[2] Shafrin, Jason. "U.S. Spends $700 Billion on Unnecessary Medical Tests." *Healthcare Economist*, November 7, 2008. http://healthcare-economist.com/2008/11/07/us-spends-700-billion-on-unnecessary-medical-tests/.

[3] Konrad, Walecia. "Medicare Fraud Victimizes Patients and Taxpayers." *The New York Times*, September 11, 2012.http://www.nytimes.com/2012/09/12/business/retirementspecial/medicare-fraud-victimizes-patients-and-taxpayers.html.

[4] McClanahan, Carolyn. "What is a Medical Loss Ratio? The Check will be in the Mail." *Forbes*. May 15, 2012. http://www.forbes.com/sites/carolynmcclana han/2012/05/15/what-is-a-medical-loss-ratio-the-check-will-be-in-the-mail/.

[5] "Top U.S. Pharmaceutical Products by Spending." *IMS HEALTH*. February 23, 2012. http://www.imshealth.com/deployed-files/ims/Global/Content/Corporate/Press percent20Room/Top-Line percent20Market percent20Data percent20& percent20Trends/2011 percent20Top-line percent20Market percent20Data/Top_Products_by_Sales.pdf

[6] Translated by King, L. W. "Hammurabi's Code of Laws." *University of Evansville*. 1997. http://eawc.evansville.edu/anthology/hammurabi.htm.

[7] Hoyert, Donna L. and Xu Jiaquan. "Deaths: Preliminary Data for 2011." *National Vital Statistics Report: Center for Disease Control* 61 no. 6 (October, 2012): 1-52.
http://www.cdc.gov/nchs/data/nvsr/nvsr61/nvsr61_06.pdf.

[8] Null, Garry et al. *Death by Medicine*. Praktikos Books, 2011, 21.

[9] Null, Garry et al. "The American Medical System is the Leading Cause of Death and Injury in the United States." *Our Civilization*. http://www.ourcivilisation.com/medicine/usamed.htm.

[10] Gray, Bradford H. *The Profit Motive and Patient Care: The Changing Accountability of Doctors and Hospitals*. Harvard University Press, 1993, 204-205.

[11] Gray, Bradford H. *The Profit Motive and Patient Care: The Changing Accountability of Doctors and Hospitals*, 184, 211.

[12] Gray, Bradford H. *The Profit Motive and Patient Care: The Changing Accountability of Doctors and Hospitals*, 204-205.

[13] Gray, Bradford H. *The Profit Motive and Patient Care: The Changing Accountability of Doctors and Hospitals*. Harvard University Press, 1993, 213.

[14] Gray, Bradford H. *The Profit Motive and Patient Care: The Changing Accountability of Doctors and Hospitals*. Harvard University Press, 1993, 220.

[15] Ezekiel, Emanuel J. *Healthcare Guaranteed: A Simple, Secure Solution for America*. PublicAffairs, 2008, 81.

[16] Gray, Bradford H. *The Profit Motive and Patient Care: The Changing Accountability of Doctors and Hospitals*. Harvard University Press, 1993, 182.

[17] Gray, Bradford H. *The Profit Motive and Patient Care: The Changing Accountability of Doctors and Hospitals*. Harvard University Press, 1993, 185.

[18] Gray, Bradford H. *The Profit Motive and Patient Care: The Changing Accountability of Doctors and Hospitals*. Harvard University Press, 1993, 187.

[19] Gray, Bradford H. *The Profit Motive and Patient Care: The Changing Accountability of Doctors and Hospitals*. Harvard University Press, 1993, 168–171.

[20] Berenson, Alex. "Incentives Limit Any Savings in Treating Cancer." *The New York Times*, June 12, 2007, sec. Business. http://www.nytimes.com/2007/06/12/business/12cancerpay.html.

[21] Melville, Nancy A. "Why Are MDs Burning Out in Record Numbers?" *Medscape News Today*, November 27, 2012. http://www.medscape.com/viewarticle/775135

[22] Chen, Pauline W. "Med Students and the Risk of Doctor Suicide." *The New York Times*, October 7, 2010, sec. Health / Views. http://www.nytimes.com/2010/10/07/health/views/07chen.html

[23] "Madeline's Story: A Real Case Demonstrating the Unfairness of Damage Caps." Citizens for Insurance Industry Reform. http://www.delcotrial.org/pages/stories.html.

[24] Black, Alexis. "Unnecessary Surgery Exposed! Why 60 percent of All Surgeries Are Medically Unjustified and How Surgeons Exploit Patients to Generate Profits." *NaturalNews.com*, October 7, 2005.

[25] Null, Gary. *Death by Medicine*. Pratikos Books, 2011.

[26] Shafrin, Jason. "U.S. Spends $700 Billion on Unnecessary Medical Tests." *Healthcare Economist*, November 7, 2008.

[27] Personal correspondence.

[28] Black, Alexis. "Unnecessary Surgery Exposed! Why 60 percent of All Surgeries Are Medically Unjustified and How Surgeons Exploit Patients to Generate Profits." *NaturalNews.com*, October 7, 2005.

[29] Ginsburg, Jack A., et al. "Achieving a High-performance Health Care System with Universal Access: What the United States Can Learn from Other Countries." *Annals of Internal Medicine* 148, no. 1 (January 1, 2008): 55–75.

[30] "Medicare Spending" *Dartmouth Atlas, Dartmouth Institute for Health Policy and Clinical Practice.* June 2011. http://www.dartmouthatlas.org/keyissues/issue.aspx?con=1339.

[31] Gawande, Atul. "The Cost Conundrum." *The New Yorker,* June 1, 2009. http://www.newyorker.com/reporting/2009/06/01/090601fa_fact_gawande.

[32] Gawande, Atul. "The Cost Conundrum." *The New Yorker,* June 1, 2009.

[33] National Health Expenditures Fact Sheet

[34] Gawande, Atul. "The Cost Conundrum." *The New Yorker,* June 1, 2009.

[35] Anderson, John W., and Larry Trivieri, eds. *Alternative Medicine: The Definitive Guide.* 2nd Updated. Celestial Arts, 2002.

[36] Black, Alexis. "Unnecessary Surgery Exposed! Why 60 percent of All Surgeries Are Medically Unjustified and How Surgeons Exploit Patients to Generate Profits." *NaturalNews.com,* October 7, 2005.

[37] Null, Gary. *The Woman's Encyclopedia of Natural Healing.* Seven Stories Press, 1996.

[38] Mayo Clinic Staff. "Coronary Bypass Surgery - Risks." Mayoclinic.com. http://www.mayoclinic.com/health/coronary-bypass-surgery/MY00087/DSECTION=risks.

[39] Mahar, Maggie. *Money-Driven Medicine: The Real Reason Health Care Costs So Much.* Collins, 2006, 42-43.

[40] Smillie, John G. *Can Physicians Manage the Quality and Costs of Health Care? The Story of the Permanente Medical Group.* McGraw-Hill, 1991.

[41] "Kaiser to Cut 1,200 Jobs in Northern California." *Sacramento Business Journal,* August 16, 2009. http://www.bizjournals.com/sacramento/stories/2009/08/17/story11.html?q=chris percent20rauber percent20kaiser.

[42] "Survey of U.S, Physicians Released; Finds Less Than 60 percent Providing Charity Care." Becker's ASC Review, September 4, 2009. http://www.beckersasc.com/news-analysis/survey-of-us-physicians-released-finds-less-than-60-providing-charity-care.html

[43] Rosenberg, Ira H., and Michael S. Backus. "Managed Care Contracting - Reimbursement Models." Managed Care Resources, Inc. http://www.mcres.com/mcrmcc03.htm.

[44] Trusted, Rosemary Dudley. "10 Things Your HMO Doctor Won't Tell You." *SmartMoney.com.* http://www.smartmoney.com/spend/family-money/10-things-your-hmo-doctor-wont-tell-you-3924/.

[45] Crane, Mark. "Funding for Graduate Medical Education Is Hotly Debated." *Medscape News* Today, August 17, 2012. http://www.medscape.com/viewarticle/769363.

[46] Metzler, Ian, et al. "The Critical State of Graduate Medical Education Funding." *Bulletin of the American College of Surgeons* 97, no. 11 (2012): 9–18.

[47] Metzler, Ian, et al. "The Critical State of Graduate Medical Education Funding." *Bulletin of the American College of Surgeons.*

[48] Iskowitz, Marc. "Pharma Slashed CME Funding Again Last Year Report." *Medical Marketing & Media,* July 25, 2012. http://www.mmm-online.com/pharma-slashed-cme-funding-again-last-year-report/article/251878/.

[49] Iskowitz, Marc. "Pharma Slashed CME Funding Again Last Year Report." *Medical Marketing & Media,* July 25, 2012. http://www.mmm-online.com/pharma-slashed-cme-funding-again-last-year-report/article/251878/.

[50] "Accreditation Council for CME Publishes 2010 Annual Report Data." August 11, 2011. http://www.accme.org/news-publications/news/accreditation-council-cme-publishes-2010-annual-report-data.

[51] Wilson, Duff. "Harvard Medical School in Ethics Quandary." *The New York Times*, March 3, 2009, sec. Business. http://www.nytimes.com/2009/03/03/business/03medschool.html.

[52] Wilson, Duff. "Harvard Medical School in Ethics Quandary." *The New York Times*, March 3, 2009, sec. Business. http://www.nytimes.com/2009/03/03/business/03medschool.html.

[53] Stein, Jeff. "Weill Cornell Dean Remains on Corporate Payrolls, Sparking Debate About Industry's Roll in Academia." *The Cornell Daily Sun*, November 30, 2012. http://cornellsun.com/section/news/content/2012/11/30/weill-cornell-dean-remains-corporate-payrolls-sparking-debate-about-.

[54] "Who Makes What." *Boston Magazine*, November 2004. http://www.bostonmagazine.com/2006/05/who-makes-what-1/.

[55] Brownlee, Shannon. "Doctors Without Borders." *The Washington Monthly*, April 2004, 38-44.

[56] Brownlee, Shannon. "Doctors Without Borders." *The Washington Monthly*, April 2004, 38-44.

[57] Harris, Gardiner. "Top Psychiatrist Didn't Report Drug Makers' Pay." *The New York Times*, October 4, 2008, sec. Health / Health Care Policy. http://www.nytimes.com/2008/10/04/health/policy/04drug.html.

[58] Harris, Gardiner. "Top Psychiatrist Didn't Report Drug Makers' Pay." *The New York Times*, October 4, 2008, sec. Health / Health Care Policy. http://www.nytimes.com/2008/10/04/health/policy/04drug.html.

[59] Post, Tim. "U of M Medical School Reorganizes; Dean Out by Summer." *Minnesota Public Radio News*, January 29, 2009. http://minnesota.publicradio.org/display/web/2009/01/29/u_of_m_medical_school_reorganizes_dean_out_by_summer.

[60] Singer, Natasha. "Senator Moves to Block Medical Ghostwriting." *The New York Times*, August 19, 2009, sec. Health / Research. http://www.nytimes.com/2009/08/19/health/research/19ethics.html.

[61] Hartocollis, Anemona. "Laurie H. Glimcher Named Dean of Weill Cornell Medical College." *The New York Times*, September 7, 2011, sec. N.Y. / Region. http://www.nytimes.com/2011/09/08/nyregion/laurie-h-glimcher-named-dean-of-weill-cornell-medical-college.html.

[62] Singer, Natasha. "Senator Moves to Block Medical Ghostwriting." *The New York Times*, August 19, 2009, sec. Health / Research. http://www.nytimes.com/2009/08/19/health/research/19ethics.html.

[63] Biley, Francis C. "The 'Sickening' Search for Health: Ivan Illich's Revised Thoughts on the Medicalization of Life and Medical Iatrogenesis." *International Journal of Holistic Healing* 10 no. 2, (May, 2010). http://ip-72-167-195-46.ip.secureserver.net/user_files/documents/ijhc/articles/Biley-10-2F.pdf.

[64] Singer, Natasha. "Senator Moves to Block Medical Ghostwriting." *The New York Times*, August 19, 2009, sec. Health / Research. http://www.nytimes.com/2009/08/19/health/research/19ethics.html.

[65] Singer, Natasha. "Senator Moves to Block Medical Ghostwriting." *The New York Times*, August 19, 2009, sec. Health / Research. http://www.nytimes.com/2009/08/19/health/research/19ethics.html.

[66] Singer, Natasha. "Medical Papers by Ghostwriters Pushed Therapy." *The New York Times*, August 5, 2009, sec. Health / Research. http://www.nytimes.com/2009/08/05/health/research/05ghost.html.

[67] Singer, Natasha. "Senator Moves to Block Medical Ghostwriting." *The New York Times*, August 19, 2009, sec. Health / Research. http://www.nytimes.com/2009/08/19/health/research/19ethics.html.

[68] Mahar, Maggie. *Money-Driven Medicine: The Real Reason Health Care Costs So Much*. Collins, 2006, 315.

[69] Mahar, Maggie. *Money-Driven Medicine: The Real Reason Health Care Costs So Much*. Collins, 2006, 315.

[70] Mahar, Maggie. *Money-Driven Medicine: The Real Reason Health Care Costs So Much*. Collins, 2006, 319.

[71] Mahar, Maggie. *Money-Driven Medicine: The Real Reason Health Care Costs So Much*. Collins, 2006, 319.

[72] Mahar, Maggie. *Money-Driven Medicine: The Real Reason Health Care Costs So Much*. Collins, 2006, 319-320.

[73] Cauchon, Dennis. "FDA Advisers Tied to Industry." *USA Today*, September 25, 2009.

[74] Harris, Gardiner. "F.D.A. Limits Role of Advisers Tied to Industry." *The New York Times*, March 22, 2007, sec. Washington. http://www.nytimes.com/2007/03/22/washington/22fda.html.

[75] Harris, Gardiner. "Ex-Head of F.D.A. Faces Criminal Inquiry." *The New York Times*, April 29, 2006, sec. Washington. http://www.nytimes.com/2006/04/29/washington/29fda.html.

[76] "Former FDA Commissioner Andrew Von Eschenbach Joins Greenleaf Health as Senior Advisor." *Reuters*, February 25, 2009. http://www.reuters.com/article/2009/02/25/idUS184309+25-Feb-2009+BW20090225.

[77] Mundy, Alicia. "New FDA Chief Must Divest Several Stock, Fund Holdings." *Wall Street Journal*, May 26, 2009, sec. Politics. http://online.wsj.com/article/SB124328188115551961.html.

[78] Birnbaum, Jeffrey H. "The Road to Riches Is Called K Street." *The Washington Post*, June 22, 2005, sec. Business. http://www.washingtonpost.com/wp-dyn/content/article/2005/06/21/AR2005062101632.html.

[79] Harris, Gardiner, and David M. Halbfinger. "F.D.A. Reveals It Fell to a Push by Lawmakers." *The New York Times*, September 25, 2009, sec. Health / Health Care Policy. http://www.nytimes.com/2009/09/25/health/policy/25knee.html.

[80] Harris, Gardiner, and David M. Halbfinger. "F.D.A. Reveals It Fell to a Push by Lawmakers." *The New York Times*, September 25, 2009, sec. Health / Health Care Policy. http://www.nytimes.com/2009/09/25/health/policy/25knee.html.

[81] Harris, Gardiner, and David M. Halbfinger. "F.D.A. Reveals It Fell to a Push by Lawmakers." *The New York Times*, September 25, 2009, sec. Health / Health Care Policy. http://www.nytimes.com/2009/09/25/health/policy/25knee.html.

[82] Willman, David. "REZULIN: Fast-Track Approval and a Slow Withdrawal." *Los Angeles Times*, December 20, 2000. http://www.latimes.com/news/nationworld/nation/la-122001rezulin,1,2676940.story.

[83] Willman, David. "REZULIN: Fast-Track Approval and a Slow Withdrawal." *Los Angeles Times*, December 20, 2000. http://www.latimes.com/news/nationworld/nation/la-122001rezulin,1,2676940.story.

[84] Lenzer, Jeanne, and Keith Epstein. "The Yaz Men: Members of FDA Panel Reviewing the Risks of Popular Bayer Contraceptive Had Industry Ties." *The Washington Monthly*, January 9, 2012. http://www.washingtonmonthly.com/ten-miles-square/2012/01/the_yaz_men_members_of_fda_pan034651.php.

[85] Lenzer, Jeanne, and Keith Epstein. "The Yaz Men: Members of FDA Panel Reviewing the Risks of Popular Bayer Contraceptive Had Industry Ties." *The Washington Monthly*, January 9, 2012. http://www.washingtonmonthly.com/ten-miles-square/2012/01/the_yaz_men_members_of_fda_pan034651.php.

[86] Colucci, Joe. "FDA: 'Intellectual' conflict of interest more serious than actual conflict." *The New Health Dialogue*, January 13, 2012. http://health.newamerica.net/blogposts/2012/fda_intellectual_conflict_of_interest_more_serious_than_actual_conflict-62350.

[87] Colucci, Joe. "FDA: 'Intellectual' conflict of interest more serious than actual conflict." *The New Health Dialogue*, January 13, 2012. http://health.newamerica.net/blogposts/2012/fda_intellectual_conflict_of_interest_more_serious_than_actual_conflict-62350.

[88] Ariadndndough. Message board comment, March 30, 2012 (11:31 a.m.), *InvestorsHub*. http://investorshub.advfn.com/boards/read_msg.aspx?message_id=73873088.

[89] Harris, Gardiner, and Benedict Carey. "Researchers Fail to Reveal Full Drug Pay." *The New York Times*, June 8, 2008, sec. US. http://www.nytimes.com/2008/06/08/us/08conflict.html.

[90] Harris, Gardiner, and Benedict Carey. "Researchers Fail to Reveal Full Drug Pay." *The New York Times*, June 8, 2008, sec. US. http://www.nytimes.com/2008/06/08/us/08conflict.html.

[91] Harris, Gardiner, and Benedict Carey. "Researchers Fail to Reveal Full Drug Pay." *The New York Times*, June 8, 2008, sec. US. http://www.nytimes.com/2008/06/08/us/08conflict.html.

[92] "Heart Test Urged Before Kids Get ADHD Drugs." *MSNBC*, April 4, 2008. http://www.msnbc.msn.com/id/24244468/ns/health-childrens_health/t/heart-test-urged-kids-get-adhd-drugs/.

[93] "Heart Test Urged Before Kids Get ADHD Drugs." *MSNBC*, April 4, 2008. http://www.msnbc.msn.com/id/24244468/ns/health-childrens_health/t/heart-test-urged-kids-get-adhd-drugs/.

[94] Wang, Shirley S. "Psychiatrists Grumble About Cardiac Testing for ADHD Drugs." *The Wall Street Journal - Health Blog*, May 5, 2008. http://blogs.wsj.com/health/2008/05/05/psychatrists-grumble-about-cardiac-testing-for-adhd-drugs/.

[95] Harris, Gardiner, and Benedict Carey. "Researchers Fail to Reveal Full Drug Pay." *The New York Times*, June 8, 2008, sec. US. http://www.nytimes.com/2008/06/08/us/08conflict.html.

[96] "Gifted and ADHD." Vanderbilt University. http://pty.vanderbilt.edu/gifted-and-adhd/.

[97] Kern, Caroline. "Prescription drug, not skate board accident, killed Clawson teen." *The Oakland Press*, April 14, 2000.

[98] "Heart Test Urged Before Kids Get ADHD Drugs." *MSNBC*, April 4, 2008. http://www.msnbc.msn.com/id/24244468/ns/health-childrens_health/t/heart-test-urged-kids-get-adhd-drugs/.

[99] "Heart Test Urged Before Kids Get ADHD Drugs." *MSNBC*, April 4, 2008. http://www.msnbc.msn.com/id/24244468/ns/health-childrens_health/t/heart-test-urged-kids-get-adhd-drugs/.

[100] "Heart Test Urged Before Kids Get ADHD Drugs." *MSNBC* April 4, 2008. http://www.msnbc.msn.com/id/24244468/ns/health-childrens_health/t/heart-test-urged-kids-get-adhd-drugs/.

[101] Jeff Madrick, "Obama & Health Care: The Straight Story," *The New York Review of Books*, June 21, 2012. http://www.nybooks.com/articles/archives/2012/jun/21/obama-and-health-care-straight-story/?pagination=false.

[102] Ryan Grim, "Internal Memo Confirms Big Giveaways In White House Deal With Big Pharma," *The Huffington Post*, September 13, 2009. http://www.huffingtonpost.com/2009/08/13/internal-memo-confirms-bi_n_258285.html

[103] Peter Baker, "Obama Was Pushed by Drug Industry, E-Mails Suggest," *The New York Times*, June 8, 2012. http://www.nytimes.com/2012/06/09/us/politics/e-mails-reveal-extent-of-obamas-deal-with-industry-on-health-care.html?pagewanted=all&_r=0.

[104] Ryan Grim, "Internal Memo Confirms Big Giveaways In White House Deal With Big Pharma," *The Huffington Post*, September 13, 2009.

[105] Richard Kirsch, *Fighting for Our Health: The Epic Battle to Make Health Care a Right in the United States,* Rockefeller Institute Press, 2009.

[106] Mahar, Maggie. *Money-Driven Medicine: The Real Reason Health Care Costs So Much*. Collins, 2006, 104.

[107] Null, Gary. *Death by Medicine*. Axios Press, 2011.

[108] Mahar, Maggie. *Money-Driven Medicine: The Real Reason Health Care Costs So Much*. Collins, 2006, 103.

[109] Akerlof, George A. "The Market for 'Lemons': Quality Uncertainty and the Market Mechanism." *The Quarterly Journal of Economics*, Vol. 84, No. 3. (Aug., 1970), 488-500.

[110] Mahar, Maggie. *Money-Driven Medicine: The Real Reason Health Care Costs So Much*. Collins, 2006, 104.

[111] Mahar, Maggie. *Money-Driven Medicine: The Real Reason Health Care Costs So Much*. Collins, 2006, 103.

[112] Noah, Timothy. "The Make-Believe Billion." *Slate*, March 3, 2011. http://www.slate.com/articles/business/the_customer/2011/03/the_makebelieve_billion.html.

[113] Public Citizen Congress Watch, "Rx R & D Myths: The Case Against the Drug Industry's R & D 'Scare Card,' " July 2001. citizen.org.

[114] Light, Donald W., and Rebecca Warburton, "Demythologizing the High Costs of Pharmaceutical Research," The London School of Economics and Political Science 1745-8552, *BioSocieties* 1-17, February 7, 2011. www.palgrave-journals.com/biosoc/.

[115] Noah, Timothy. "The Make-Believe Billion." *Slate*, March 3, 2011. http://www.slate.com/articles/business/the_customer/2011/03/the_makebelieve_billion.html.

[116] Light, Donald W., and J. R. Lexchin. "Pharmaceutical Research and Development: What Do We Get for All That Money?" *BMJ* 345, August 7, 2012: e4348–e4348.

[117] Garde, Damian. "Top 10 Pharma CEO Salaries of 2011." *FiercePharma,* May 1, 2012. http://www.fiercepharma.com/special-reports/top-10-pharma-ceo-salaries-2011/top-10-pharma-ceo-salaries-2011.

[118] Garde, Damian. "Top 10 Pharma CEO Salaries of 2011." *FiercePharma,* May 1, 2012. http://www.fiercepharma.com/special-

reports/top-10-pharma-ceo-salaries-2011/top-10-pharma-ceo-salaries-2011.

[119] Angell, Marcia. *The Truth About the Drug Companies: How They Deceive Us and What to Do About It.* Random House Trade Paperbacks, 2005, 12.

[120] Edwards, Jim. "12 Pharma CEOs Who Can't Stop Vacationing on the Company Jet." *CBS News,* April 15, 2011. http://www.cbsnews.com/8301-505123_162-42847982/12-pharma-ceos-who-cant-stop-vacationing-on-the-company-jet/.

[121] Public Citizen Congress Watch. "Rx R & D Myths: The Case Against the Drug Industry's R & D 'Scare Card.'" July 2001. citizen.org.

[122] U.S. Congress, Office of Technology Assessment, *Pharmaceutical R&D: Costs, Risks, and Rewards,* OTA-H-522 (Washington, DC: U.S. Government Printing Office, February 1993).

[123] Public Citizen Congress Watch. "Rx R & D Myths: The Case Against the Drug Industry's R & D 'Scare Card.'" July 2001. citizen.org.

[124] "WHO | Pharmaceutical Industry." *World Health Organization.* http://www.who.int/trade/glossary/story073/en/index.html.

[125] Crosett, Kathy. "Pharmaceutical Industry Revenue to Grow in 2011." *Marketing Forecast,* October 29, 2010. http://www.marketing-forecast.com/archives/8000/.

[126] Mahar, Maggie, Money-Driven Medicine: The Real Reason Health Care Costs so Much (New York: HarperCollins, 2006), 61–65.

[127] Aldrich, Nancy. "Medicare Fraud Estimates: A Moving Target?" *The Sentinel,* May 2010. www.smpresource.org.

[128] "The Price of Excess: Identifying Waste in Healthcare Spending." *PwC.* April 2008. http://www.pwc.com/us/en/healthcare/publications/the-price-of-excess.jhtml.

[129] "Where Can $700 Billion in Waste be Cut Annually from the U.S. Healthcare System?" *Thomson Reuters*, October 2009.

[130] "Where Can $700 Billion in Waste be Cut Annually from the U.S. Healthcare System?" *Thomson Reuters*, October 2009.

[131] Rush, Brittany. "Where the Money Goes." Health Care Cost Monitor, March 3, 2011. http://healthcarecostmonitor.thehastingscenter.org/brittanyrush/where-the-money-goes/.

[132] Aldrich, Nancy. "Medicare Fraud Estimates: A Moving Target?" *The Sentinel*, May 2010. http://www.smpresource.org/Content/NavigationMenu/AboutSMPs/MedicareFraudEstimatesAMovingTarget/Medicare_Fraud_Estimates.pdf.

[133] "GlaxoSmithKline to Plead Guilty and Pay $3 Billion to Resolve Fraud Allegations and Failure to Report Safety Data - Largest Health Care Fraud Settlement in U.S. History." Department of Justice, July 2, 2012.

[134] "Justice Department Announces Largest Health Care Fraud Settlement in its History - Pfizer To Pay $2.3 Billion For Fraudulent Marketing." Department of Justice, September 2, 2009.

[135] "Abbott Labs to Pay $1.5 Billion to Resolve Criminal & Civil Investigations of Off-label Promotion of Depakote - Company Maintained Specialized Sales Force to Market Drug for Off Label Purposes; Targeted Elderly Dementia Patients in Nursing Homes." Department of Justice, May 7, 2012.

[136] "Eli Lilly and Company Agrees to Pay $1.415 Billion to Resolve Allegations of Off-label Promotion of Zyprexa - $515 Million Criminal Fine Is Largest Individual Corporate Criminal Fine in History; Civil Settlement up to $800 Million." Department of Justice, January 15, 2009.

[137] "TAP Pharmaceutical Products Inc. and Seven Others Charged With Health Care Crimes; Company Agrees to Pay $875 Million to Settle Charges." Department of Justice, October 3, 2001.

[138] "Amgen Inc. Pleads Guilty to Federal Charge in Brooklyn, NT.; Pays $762 Million to Resolve Criminal Liability and False Claims Act Allegations." Department of Justice, December 19, 2012.

[139] "GlaxoSmithKline to Plead Guilty & Pay $750 Million to Resolve Criminal and Civil Liability Regarding Manufacturing Deficiencies at Puerto Rico Plant." Department of Justice, October 26, 2010.

[140] "Serono to Pay $704 Million for the Illegal Marketing of AIDS Drug." Department of Justice, October 17, 2005.

[141] "Merck to Pay More than $650 Million to Resolve Claims of Fraudulent Price Reporting and Kickbacks." Department of Justice, February 7, 2008.

[142] "Office of the Attorney General." November 7, 2008. justice.gov.

[143] "Department of Justice Recovers $3 Billion in False Claims Cases in Fiscal Year 2010." Department of Justice, November 22, 2010.

[144] Bronstein, Scott, and Drew Griffin. "Dialysis Company Accused of Giant Medicare Fraud." *CNN*, November 30, 2012. http://www.cnn.com/2012/11/30/health/medicare-fraud-case/index.html.

[145] "Doctor Sentenced to 16 Years in Prison for Performing Unnecessary Surgeries on Healthy Patients in $154 Million Medical Insurance Fraud Scheme - Issued by the Orange County District Attorney's Office." May 8, 2009. https://www.ftb.ca.gov/aboutFTB/press/archive/2009/09_27.shtml

[146] "Doctor Sentenced to 16 Years in Prison for Performing Unnecessary Surgeries on Healthy Patients in $154 Million Medical Insurance Fraud Scheme - Issued by the Orange County District Attorney's Office." May 8, 2009.

[147] "Doctor Sentenced to 16 Years in Prison for Performing Unnecessary Surgeries on Healthy Patients in $154 Million Medical Insurance Fraud Scheme - Issued by the Orange County District Attorney's Office." May 8, 2009.

[148] Herzlinger, Regina. *Who Killed Health Care: America's $2 Trillion Medical Problem and the Consumer Driven Cure*. McGraw-Hill, 2007, 209-210.

[149] Jennifer Prah Ruger, "Toward a Theory of a Right to Health: Capability and Incompletely Theorized Agreements," 294.

[150] Hans V. Hogerzeil, "Is access to essential medicines as part of the fulfilment of the right to health enforceable through the courts?" 309.

[151] Riedel, Eibe. "The Human Right to Health: Conceptual Foundations," in *Swiss Human Rights Book vol 3 Realizing the Right Health*. ed. Andrew Clapham and Mary Robinson, (Zurich: University of Zurich Political Pilosophy, 2009), 21-39. http://www.swisshumanrightsbook.com/SHRB/shrb_03_files/01_453_Riedel.pdf, 26.

[152] Ruger, Jennifer Prah. "Toward a Theory of a Right to Health: Capability and Incompletely Theorized Agreements." *Yale Journal of Law & the Humanities* 18, (July 2006): 273-326. http://www.bvsde.paho.org/bvsacd/cd63/Towardtheory.pdf, 282.

[153] Burney, Robert M.D. "Has Health Care Become a Commodity." *Advanced Web Executive Insight.* February 18, 2011. http://healthcare-executive-insight.advanceweb.com/Columns/Eye-on-Quality/Has-Healthcare-Become-a-Commodity.aspx.

[154] Woolhandler, Steffie, Terry Campbell, and David U. Himmelstein. "Costs of Health Care Administration in the United States and Canada." *The New England Journal of Medicine* 349, no. 8 (2003): 768–775.

[155] "Medical Coder Salary." Indeed.com. http://www.indeed.com/salary/Medical-Coder.html.

[156] Konrad, Walecia. "Medicare Fraud Victimizes Patients and Taxpayers." *The New York Times*, September 11, 2012.

[157] Kliff, Sarah. "Maybe Medical School Debt Isn't the Problem." *The Washington Post - Blogs*, May 30, 2012. http://www.washingtonpost.com/blogs/wonkblog/post/maybe-medical-school-debt-isnt-the-problem/2012/05/30/gJQA2ab41U_blog.html.

[158] Hibma, Pierce. "Real Life Example of Medical School Debt." *KevinMD.com*. http://www.kevinmd.com/blog/2011/04/real-life-medical-school-debt.html.

[159] Harrison, J.D. "Health-care Law Driving Doctors Away from Small Practices, Toward Hospital Employment." *Washington Post*, July 19, 2012. http://articles.washingtonpost.com/2012-07-19/business/35489044_1_primary-care-physicians-health-care-reform-law-accountable-care-organizations.

[160] Russakoff, Dale. "Old Age in America, by the Numbers." *The New York Times - The New Old Age Blog*. July 21, 2010. http://newoldage.blogs.nytimes.com/2010/07/21/aging-in-america-how-its-changing/.

[161] *The Long-Term Budget Outlook.* Congressional Budget Office (CBO Publication No. 2883). Washington, DC: U.S. Government Printing Office, 2008.

[162] *Building a Better Health Care System: Specifications for Reform*. National Coalition on Health Care, 2004.

[163] "Censo de Poblacíon y Vivienda 2010." Instituto Nacional de Estadística y Geografía (INEGI), 2010.

[164] Abelson, Reed. "Insurers Push Plans That Limit Health Choices." *The New York Times*, July 17, 2010, sec. Business. http://www.nytimes.com/2010/07/18/business/18choice.html.

[165] Dube, Arindrajit. "Productivity Impact of Health Care Reform in California." Institute for Labor and Employment, University of California, Berkeley, August 2003.

[166] "Healthy Workforce 2010 and Beyond," Partnership for Prevention, 2010.

[167] Reid, T.R. *The Healing of America: A Global Quest for Better, Cheaper, and Fairer Health Care*. Penguin Books, 2009, 28.

[168] "John Boehner Says U.S. Health Care System is Best in the World." *Politfact*. July 1, 2012. http://www.politifact.com/truth-o-meter/statements/2012/jul/05/john-boehner/john-boehner-says-us-health-care-system-best-world/.

[169] Tanner, Michael. "Opposing View: Despite Flaws, U.S. Health Care the Best." *USA Today*. October 17, 2011. http://usatoday30.usatoday.com/news/opinion/story/2011-10-17/USA-health-care/50807584/1.

[170] Reid, T.R. *The Healing of America: A Global Quest for Better, Cheaper, and Fairer Health Care*, 29.

[171] "The World Health Report 2000 - Health Systems: Improving Performance." *World Health Organization (WHO)*. http://www.who.int/whr/2000/en/whr00_en.pdf.

[172] "Health Expenditures Per Capita 2009" *Global Health Facts*. http://www.globalhealthfacts.org/data/topic/map.aspx?ind=66.

[173] "Health Expenditures Per Capita 2009" *Global Health Facts*.

[174] "Factbox: U.S. Healthcare by the Numbers." *Reuters*. June 28, 2012. http://www.reuters.com/article/2012/06/28/us-usa-healthcare-court-numbers-idUSBRE85R0XN20120628.

[175] Hinckley, David. "Infant Death Haunts Grim 'Babyland' on ABC's '20/20' Special." *NY Daily News*. August 21, 2008. http://www.nydailynews.com/entertainment/tv-movies/infant-death-haunts-grim-babyland-abc-20-20-special-article-1.315458.

[176] Klein, Ezra. "The Health of Nations." *The American Prospect*, April 22, 2007. http://prospect.org/article/health-nations.

[177] Klein, Ezra. "The Health of Nations." *The American Prospect*, April 22, 2007. http://prospect.org/article/health-nations.

[178] Klein, Ezra. "The Health of Nations." *The American Prospect*, April 22, 2007. http://prospect.org/article/health-nations.

[179] Valdez, Veronica M. "China's De-socialized Medicine." *Foreign Policy*. June 11, 2009. http://www.foreignpolicy.com/articles/2009/06/10/chinas_de_socialized_medicine.

[180] Hahn, Robert, and Peter Passell. "China's Healthcare System Thrives Despite Slowing Economy." *U.S. News - Economic Intelligence,* June 11, 2012. http://www.usnews.com/opinion/blogs/economic-intelligence/2012/06/11/chinas-healthcare-system-thrives-despite-slowing-economy.

[181] Hougaard, Jens Leth, Lars Peter Østerdal, and Yi Yu. "The Chinese Healthcare System: Structure, Problems and Challenges." *Applied Health Economics and Health Policy* 9, no. 1 (January 2011): 1–13.

[182] Hahn, Robert, and Peter Passell. "China's Healthcare System Thrives Despite Slowing Economy." *U.S. News - Economic Intelligence,* June 11, 2012. http://www.usnews.com/opinion/blogs/economic-intelligence/2012/06/11/chinas-healthcare-system-thrives-despite-slowing-economy.

[183] Hahn, Robert, and Peter Passell. "China's Healthcare System Thrives Despite Slowing Economy." *U.S. News - Economic Intelligence,* June 11, 2012. http://www.usnews.com/opinion/blogs/economic-intelligence/2012/06/11/chinas-healthcare-system-thrives-despite-slowing-economy.

[184] Notle, Ellen. McKee, C. Martin. "Measuring the Health of Nations: Updating and Earlier." *Health Affairs* 27, no. 1 (January/February 2008): 58-71.http://content.healthaffairs.org/content/27/1/58.full.

[185] Klein, Ezra. "The Health of Nations." *The American Prospect,* April 22, 2007. http://prospect.org/article/health-nations.

[186] Dutton, Paul V. *Differential Diagnoses: A Comparative History of Health Care Problems and Solutions in the United States and France*. 1st ed. ILR Press, 2012.

[187] Durand-Zaleski, Isabelle. "The French Health Care System, 2009." *International Profiles of Health Care Systems.* Ed. The Commonwealth Fund. New York, 2009. 23-27.

[188] Ed. Thompson, Sarah and Reed, Sarah Jane. "International Profiles of Health Care Systems, 2012" *The Commonwealth Fund.* http://www.commonwealthfund.org/~/media/Files/Publications/Fund percent20Report/2011/Nov/1562_Squires_Intl_Profiles_2011_11_10.pdf, 7.

[189] Greb, Stefan, et. al. "Free choice of sickness funds in regulated competition: evidence from Germany and The Netherlands" *Health Policy* 60, no. 3 (June 2002): 235-254.http://nvl002.nivel.nl/postprint/PPpp1334.pdf, 3.

[190] Ed. Sarah Thompson and Sara Jane Reed, *International Profiles of Health Care Systems, 2012*, 7.

[191] "Structure of the German Health Care System." *American Institute for Contemporary German Studies*, March 8, 2012. http://www.aicgs.org/issue/structure-of-the-german-health-care-system/.

[192] Frank, Michael, et al. "Health Care Industry in Germany." *Columbia University School of Continuing Education*, 2012. http://ce.columbia.edu/files/ce/pdf/actu/actu-germany.pdf, 1.

[193] "Unicef Progress Report 2012." *Unicef.* 2012. http://www.apromiserenewed.org/files/APR_Progress_Report_2012_final_web3.pdf, 13.

[194] Michael Frank et. al, "Health Care Industry in Germany," 4.

[195] Boyle, Sean. "The UK Health Care System." *London School of Economics Health and Social Care,* February 2008. http://www.commonwealthfund.org/usr_doc/UK_Country_Profile_2008.pdf.

[196] Smith, Peter C., and Nick York. "Quality Incentives: The Case Of U.K. General Practitioners." *Health Affairs* 23, no. 3 (May 1, 2004): 112–118.

[197] Global Health Facts.

[198] "World Health Statistics 2012," *WHO.*

[199] Klein, Ezra. "The Health of Nations." *The American Prospect*, April 22, 2007. http://prospect.org/article/health-nations.

[200] Jurd, Adam. "Expenditure on Healthcare in the UK, 1997-2010." *United Kingdom Office for National Statistics*, May 2, 2012. http://www.ons.gov.uk/ons/dcp171766_264293.pdf, 5.

Made in the USA
Las Vegas, NV
03 November 2026

57424185R00098